HOW TO CHOOSE & USE

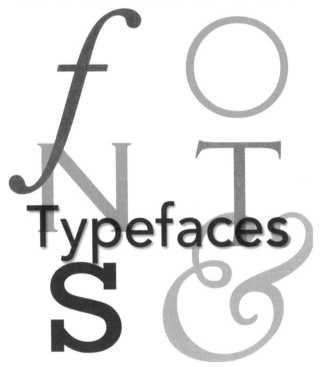

f O N T S Typefaces &

Publisher and Creative Director: Nick Wells
Project Editor: Polly Prior
Art Director and Layout Design: Mike Spender
Digital Design and Production: Chris Herbert
General Editor: Tony Seddon
Proofreader: Dawn Laker
Indexer: Helen Snaith

FLAME TREE PUBLISHING
6 Melbray Mews
London SW6 3NS
United Kingdom

Images courtesy of Shutterstock and © the following photographers: iulias: 4, 216; Trinet Uzun: 6; puhhha: 7; iunewind: 8; racorn: 9; Space Chimp: 11; Galyamin Sergej: 13; exopixel: 20; NorGal: 21; Rashevskyi Viacheslav: 23; baranq: 24; zlikovec: 30; Brian A Jackson: 36; baranq: 43; Alice Day: 44; Thinglass: 45; Diego Cervo: 49; schatzy: 52; ra2studio: 55; kurhan: 61; igor.stevanovic: 62; Niloo: 66; sheff: 77; Pushish Images: 79; vic dd: 81; nrey: 83; Pressmaster: 84, 232; racorn: 93; ra2studio: 98; Yeamake: 103; Vasilius: 104; www.BillionPhotos.com: 106, 195; scyther5: 107, 114; RedKoala: 108; Neuevector : 116; Monkey Business Images: 123; Noci: 131; Jennifer Stone: 134; Khakimullin Aleksandr: 138; r.classen: 139; R Weir Works: 141; Petr Lerch: 143 (b); Family Business: 145; Pablo Rogat: 148; koya979: 150; r.classen: 152; robert_s: 165; dreamerve: 167; Bohbeh: 168; inxti: 172; GanbareNippon: 185; sahua d: 186 (t); Alonso Aguilar: 187; donatas1205: 188; Stocked House Studio: 190; studioVin: 192; kozirsky: 197; Federico Rostagno: 206; disq: 207; Eugenio Marongiu: 218; szefei: 228 (t); mik ulyannikov: 230; wavebreakmedia: 225, 245 (b); Diego Cervo: 251 (t); Dudarev Mikhail: 252.

All product image shots courtesy of and ©: Atlas Foundry: 95; Process Type Foundry: 96; Colophon Foundry: 97; Font Haus: 98; Wood Type Image: 99 (t); Typekit: 99 (b); fontspring.com: 100; IKEA: 144; easyjet: 143; University of Chicago Press: 156 (t); Harpercollins Canada: 156 (b); Stereotype Design: 158; Pears Soap: 159; Macdonalds: 160; Intermarche: 161 (l); Intermarche: 161 (r); Font Deck: 147; www.semplepress.co.uk: 228 (b); Neville Brody/ Do The Green Thing: 226.

All other images courtesy of the authors.

ISBN 978-1-78361-708-1

1 3 5 7 9 10 8 6 4 2

Manufactured in China

HOW TO CHOOSE & USE

Typefaces

DIGITAL | PRINT
COMICS | BOOKS
WEB | SMARTPHONES

TONY SEDDON (GENERAL EDITOR)

ANDREA PENNOYER | SAM HAMPTON-SMITH

DAVID WOODWARD | AMBAR GALAN

FLAME TREE
PUBLISHING

CONTENTS

INTRODUCTION

So what's the big deal about choosing a typeface? You simply go to the font menu on your computer and choose Arial for plain text, Times New Roman for letters to the bank manager, and Comic Sans for those fun invitations to weekend barbecues.

THOUSANDS OF TYPEFACES

I'm being flippant, of course (Comic Sans, really?), but despite the thousands of typefaces available, those three are very often the only ones people consider. But it doesn't have to be that way, and you don't have to be a designer to benefit from increasing your knowledge about typefaces beyond the limits of those chosen by the folk at Microsoft and Apple.

NOT SO FUNNY

Like many others in my profession, I'm in constant peril of becoming a typeface snob. I quipped unkindly about Comic Sans a moment ago – in actual fact, it is a very legible typeface, particularly when used onscreen (which, incidentally, was the original goal of its designer, Vincent Connare). It is mainly because the font is so ubiquitous, and because it has been used inappropriately on so many occasions, that it has picked up such a dubious reputation.

The typeface has unadvisably appeared on everything from curriculum vitae (wrong!), to posters warning of serious crimes (no!) and even obituary notices (I'm speechless). Just type 'comic sans used badly' into Google and you'll see what I mean. If Comic Sans hadn't been included with every PC sold since 1995, things could have been very different.

THE AIM OF THIS BOOK

What we wish to achieve with this book is to expand your understanding of what typeface options are out there, and to explain how you can use and combine them appropriately in different kinds of typographic design projects.

Choosing a typeface is a little like picking out what you want to wear; you look along the rail in your wardrobe and choose something that's sombre, or loud, or classy, or casual, depending on what activity you have in mind. Typefaces are chosen for similar reasons. They can be legible so they're clearly read and understood; they can jump off the page or screen to scream a gaudy message; they can be both sophisticated and impactful; or they can be laid-back and unobtrusive.

Furthermore, it is rare that anyone dons exactly the same style of clothing every day. You may wear a suit to work but you're unlikely to choose the same outfit to head down to the beach. It is the same with typefaces – there are sound choices for every occasion but, unless you're a seasoned professional, you won't necessarily know instinctively which to choose in the same way you'd know which shirt to wear.

MAKING THE RIGHT CHOICE

So, what are the best typefaces or the best typeface combinations? I'm afraid that's an impossible question to answer outright, because it always depends on the nature of the project you're using them for. There are lots of principles and basic rules (which we talk about in chapters two and three) that can help you to make typeface choices, so I would urge you to read those chapters fully before you jump to the later sections, which provide typeface suggestions for a variety of scenarios. However, choosing typefaces is a very subjective process and, as the saying goes, 'One man's meat is another man's poison.'

Personal choice varies considerably between designers and, indeed, between non-designers. Our suggestions for typeface choice are merely suggestions – they can be no more than that – but they're intended to give you the tools to inform your own choices. Ultimately, if you look at a typeface or combination of typefaces and think, 'They look great together,' there's a good chance that you're right.

THE STORY OF FONTS

THE EARLIEST TYPE

The history of fonts and how we've arrived at the high-tech digital versions we use today could fill this entire book, but we'll attempt to condense it down to a few pages.

IN THE BEGINNING ...

Anyone with a passing interest in the history of printed type may initially think of a fellow by the name of Johannes Gutenberg, who lived and worked in the German town of Mainz in the mid-fifteenth century. But the real story begins around 1,200 years earlier, in China.

Movable type is the term commonly applied to any system that allows words to be assembled and printed from individual reusable characters, known as sorts, and the Chinese were

Above: The printing press originated by German Johannes (Johann) Gutenberg in the fifteenth century was used without any significant change until the twentieth century.

experimenting with a form of movable type using ceramic and metal tiles as early as AD 220. However, they faced a couple of big problems which they never managed to resolve: the wrong kind of ink and too many characters. Their inks were water-based, so wouldn't stick to the ceramic tiles and their ideogrammatic alphabet, which contains thousands of individual characters, was simply too challenging to manufacture by hand, so their experiments with movable type were set aside.

Above: Set in ALOT Gutenberg, this is a faithful digital reproduction of Gutenberg's original type created by the Alter Littera type foundry.

Movable Type Arrives

By the fifteenth century, however, a couple of important factors had dramatically increased the commercial interest in printed type. The entrepreneurs of the day were alert to the fact that better levels of education meant more people could actually read – as is the case today, anyone who wanted to get on in life needed to master a basic level of linguistic skill – and the demand for printed material in the form of books or pamphlets grew ever higher. Additionally, the techniques employed to manufacture paper had improved significantly, so a relatively cheap alternative to extremely expensive vellum finally became available.

THE FIRST BOOK

At long last, the infant printing industry had a marketplace for its product, and this is where our friend Gutenberg comes in. He was a businessman with his fingers in several pies – not all of them strictly above board, by all accounts – and he's credited with the invention of the first workable movable type system. At least, the evidence points to him; there were others who laid claim to the invention at the time, but Gutenberg gets the glory, principally because of his famous *42-line Bible*, the first book to be printed with movable type in Western Europe. Incidentally, it is called the *42-line Bible* because there are 42 lines of type per page.

Left: A page from Gutenberg's *42-line Bible*. Coloured illuminations were added by hand after the main body of the text had been printed using movable type.

THE FIRST FONTS

At this time, the idea of designing fonts still was not a priority. The typeface used by Gutenberg was designed to look like the handwritten script popular in Germany in the fifteenth century, a style known as Blackletter. His readers would have struggled to decipher any other style of typeface, because they were used to reading Blackletter, so Gutenberg simply created a typeface that looked like handwriting. As a hard-nosed businessman, he was concerned principally with the commercial viability of the project; he wanted to make as much money as possible, and the idea of the design and development of a new typeface was probably the last thing on his mind.

Above: Although this is a modern version, this Adobe Jenson font is based on the first typeface to feature roman letterforms.

Then in 1470, something revolutionary happened. A Venice-based French engraver named Nicolas Jenson cut what is widely regarded as the first movable type to feature roman letterforms. This was effectively the beginning of typeface design, because Jenson's fonts didn't mimic handwriting. His design still carried attributes similar to calligraphic lettering, and it is categorized as a Humanist

Quidā eius libros nō ipſius eſſe ſed Dionyſii &Zophiri co lophoniorū tradunt:qui iocādi cauſa cōſcribentes ei ut diſ ponere idoneo dederunt.Fuerunt autē Menippi ſex. Prīus qui de lydis ſcripſit:Xanthūqʒ breuiauit.Secūdus hic ipſe. Tertius ſtratonicus ſophiſta.Quartus ſculptor . Quintus & ſextus pictores:utroſqʒ memorat apollodorus.Cynici au tem uolumina tredecī ſunt.Neniæ:teſtamenta:epiſtolæ cō poſitæ ex deorum pſona ad phyſicos & mathematicos grā‐ maticoſqʒ:& epicuri fœtus:& eas quæ ab ipſis religioſe co‐ luntur imagines:& alia.

Above: An example of Nicolas Jenson's archetypal roman typeface, from the *Laertis*, published in Venice *c.* 1475.

typeface, but it heralded a new era for real typeface design. Font categorizations are a useful element to consider when choosing fonts, and we talk about those categories in more detail on pages 58–61.

Above: This modern Monotype Bembo Book face is based on the late-fifteenth-century Venetian Bembo typeface, which was much easier to read than other, earlier romans.

Above: Garamond is considered to be one of the most easily readable of the serif typefaces; shown here is a sample of the modern version of the face, Adobe Garamond.

TYPEFACE DESIGN BEGINS

As little as 15 years after Jenson, typeface design was already becoming more refined, and a famous typeface, which we now know as Bembo, was cut by the Italian Francesco Griffo in around 1495, under the direction of printer Aldus Manutius. This was the first Old Style serif, featuring fewer calligraphic qualities than the earlier Humanist serifs, and to this day, it is a popular choice, especially for book design projects. The earliest italic fonts were also cut around this time by Manutius and Griffo.

Another famous Old Style serif to emerge during this period, Garamond, was first cut in 1532 by the Frenchman Claude Garamond, and it has spawned a raft of similar faces over the years. Garamond should be very familiar to most people today, because it is included with many computer systems and popular applications, such as Microsoft Office.

Ubiquitous Caslon

Old Style serifs dominated typeface design for the next 200 years. In Britain, an enormously important Old Style named Caslon appeared in 1725 and became the principal typeface used throughout the developed world. At one time, a common expression among printers when selecting a font was, 'When in doubt, use Caslon.' It was particularly popular in the American colonies, and the Declaration of Independence is typeset in Caslon. Then in 1757, a new kind of constructed typeface appeared – Baskerville – designed by businessman John Baskerville, and cut by John Handy.

All About Baskerville

Baskerville is known as a Transitional serif and is less calligraphic than anything that came before it, with a much higher contrast (the difference between the thickest and thinnest parts of the strokes that make up each character). Baskerville was able to carry off his typographic feat through his work in improving the technology he used to print his publications; he invented a thicker and blacker ink and he used wove paper, which had a flatter surface that didn't break up the finer details of the characters. The typeface was so radical that some readers complained about the fineness of the characters 'being too thin and narrow, hurt the eye...'.

Above: Caslon is considered to be the first original English typeface; the modern Adobe Caslon face is pictured here.

Above: Shown here is ITC New Baskerville, a modern typeface based on Baskerville, the original elegant eighteenth-century Transitional serif.

R g

Above: This modern Monotype Bembo Book face is based on the late-fifteenth-century Venetian Bembo typeface, which was much easier to read than other, earlier romans.

Above: Garamond is considered to be one of the most easily readable of the serif typefaces; shown here is a sample of the modern version of the face, Adobe Garamond.

Didone Modern

These detractors were clearly not prepared for what was to come next – the beautiful serif typefaces designed from the 1790s onwards by the likes of the Italian Giambattista Bodoni and the Frenchman Firmin Didot. Their typefaces featured a huge amount of contrast in the strokes, with extremes of thick and thin. Bodoni, in particular, admired Baskerville's work, but took the refinement even further, creating the style that we now know as Didone, or Modern.

THE INTRODUCTION OF LICENSING

By the mid-nineteenth century, the wonderful Slab serif style of typeface had become popular, particularly for use in those familiar Victorian playbill-style posters that grace the walls of many a London public house. Clarendon, designed in 1845 for the R. Besley & Co. type foundry in London, was one of the first typefaces of this kind, and it lays claim to being the first ever typeface to carry a patent. By now, competing type foundries had realized how easy it was for rivals to copy their unique typeface designs, and the idea of font licensing was born, where other foundries could manufacture a typeface with permission from the holder of the original design patent – and for a cut of the profits, of course.

THE MODERN ERA

So, by the end of the nineteenth century, the idea of the modern typeface was more or less fully formed. From this point onwards, typeface design was increasingly driven by the development of printing technology, and mechanized typesetting arrived in the form of two different hot metal machines: the Linotype and the Monotype. The term 'hot metal' is derived from the fact that after each print run, the metal used to cast the type was melted down and reused for the next job.

Linotype and Monotype

The Linotype cast solid lines of text on a single slug of metal and took its name – Line o' Type – from this. The Monotype cast individual sorts, which were mechanically assembled using a clever punched-tape

Right: The Linotype (Line o' Type) machine revolutionized the newspaper industry, in particular, as its superior speed suited the fast turnaround of daily editions.

system. Both machines were able to set type at a speed far greater than the old method, where compositors assembled lines of type by hand, picking individual sorts from special type cases. The rapid increase in output produced an even greater demand for new and unique typefaces, some of which have become household names. Typefaces such as Times New Roman (1932) and Helvetica (1957) have become so familiar that their names are synonymous with the styles themselves; for example, non-typographers often look at any serif typeface and call it a Times New Roman font.

DIGITAL BENEFITS

Since the 1980s and the beginning of the digital revolution, the classic typeface designs have prevailed, but there are now literally thousands of new typefaces to choose from too. The latest digital font technology, OpenType, allows each individual

Above Right: The Carpenter (Fenotype) is a great example of an OpenType font with plenty of alternative glyphs, allowing a huge range of character combinations to be created automatically as you type.

Above: Early Apple Macintosh computers quickly gained popularity with the design industry because of the built-in graphic capabilities and user-friendly interface.

font file to contain no fewer than 65,536 individual characters or glyphs, so typographers and designers can achieve amazing results very quickly using the font's built-in contextual character substitution, combined with the right page-layout software.

We talk in more depth about the ways you can choose and use digital fonts over the course of the following pages, but it is important to bear in mind that many of the best typeface designs emerging today still closely reference the work of talented craftsmen such as Jenson, Griffo, Baskerville and Bodoni.

PRINCIPLES

THE PRINCIPLES

This aim of this chapter is to give you some background on a range of basic typographic principles that have been developed over many years by designers and typographers. Some of them relate specifically to the design of the typefaces themselves, while others are concerned closely with the way designers use the fonts in practice.

ALWAYS READ THE TEXT

The first thing to say is, please don't skip this chapter because you think it's irrelevant. It's true that, later in the book, there are a lot of suggested typeface options and combinations for all sorts of situations that you may find yourself in when putting a project together. However, they're there as much to inspire you as they are to provide you with an off-the-peg

solution. The typefaces we've suggested may not be available in your collection, so you need to understand why the authors made their choices, so you can make informed decisions of your own, using fonts that you do own.

Learn Something New

Whether you're a professional graphic designer, a recent design graduate, or a non-designer with an interest in typography and typefaces, some knowledge of these principles will serve you well in your creative endeavours.

LEGIBILITY & READABILITY

You might think that legibility and readability are the same thing; if you can read text, that means it's legible, and if it's legible, you can read it. Well, that's a fair argument, but there are key differences that set the two definitions apart, and knowing those differences can form the backbone of many typeface decisions.

LEGIBILITY

Let's start with legibility. This is essentially the measure of how easy (or difficult) it is to distinguish separate characters from one another in any given font. For example, the rounded shape of an 'o' and an 'e' may appear alike in running text, as may an 'l' and an 'i'. As the designer, you have no influence over what the characters of a font look like – this is the responsibility of the typeface's original designer – so to achieve good legibility, your role consists of knowing which attributes to look for when choosing a typeface.

There's a general acceptance among designers that the most legible typefaces are those that don't shout 'Look at me!' but rather get on with the job of providing a clear visual experience. The reader should see the words first rather than be distracted by the appearance of the typeface. It's a fairly common mistake for inexperienced designers to pick a typeface for running text because they think it has personality or because they like the look of the fancy

Above: Novelty typefaces like Trixie, designed to look like an antique typewriter font, can be fun and have their place, but they're often not the most legible option.

details in the serifs or strokes. Save this style of typeface for attention-grabbing headlines or novelty projects, and go for something much cleaner and elegantly understated if you want your text to be legible.

What to Look For

There are a couple of key features to look out for when identifying a highly legible font. The first and probably the most effective feature is a large x-height (*see* The Anatomy of Type on pages 56–57 for a definition). The proportions afforded by a larger x-height allows character shapes to be defined more clearly, making them easier to recognize when read quickly. However, the x-height shouldn't be too similar in size to the cap height or the length of ascenders and descenders, because that may compromise legibility.

There are various theories about which combination of proportions works best, but based on the findings of the well-known eighteenth-century French typefounder Pierre Simon Fournier, if the x-height compares with the length of ascenders by a ratio of around 3:2, legibility should be enhanced.

Ilieo Ilieo

Above: News Gothic on the left and Garamond on the right are both considered to be legible typefaces. However, look how much easier it is to distinguish from one another the characters of Garamond which are represented here. On the other hand, News Gothic has a larger x-height which will aid legibility.

Serif Versus Sans Serif

Another key feature to spot is the overall simplicity of the character shapes. A long-held school of thought maintains that simpler letterforms provide a greater degree of legibility, which raises the ever-present discussion of whether serifs or sans serifs are better for running text. Serifs were traditionally regarded as more legible because the details in the letterforms helped improve character recognition, which in turn helped to guide the reader's eye along each line of text. Once the popularity of sans serif typefaces increased during the early half of the twentieth century, the theory switched to the notion that sans serif typefaces were easier to read because of their simpler forms, although a piggyback theory maintained they caused an increase in eye fatigue over longer passages of text.

There was a thin, crisp, continuous patter from somewhere in the heart of that crawling bank. The cloud was within fifty yards of where we lay, and we glared at it, all three, uncertain what horror was about to break from the heart of it. I was at Holmes's elbow, and I glanced for an instant at his face. It was pale and exultant, his eyes shining brightly in the moonlight. But suddenly they started forward in a rigid, fixed stare, and his lips parted in amazement. At the same instant Lestrade gave a yell of terror and threw himself face downward upon the ground. I sprang to my feet, my inert hand grasping my pistol, my mind paralyzed by the dreadful shape which had sprung out upon us from the shadows of the fog. A hound it was, an enormous coal-black hound, but not such a hound as mortal eyes have ever seen. Fire burst from its open mouth, its eyes glowed with a smouldering glare, its muzzle and hackles and dewlap were outlined in flickering flame. Never in the delirious dream of a disordered brain could anything more savage, more appalling, more hellish be conceived than that dark form and savage face which broke upon us out of the wall of fog.

There was a thin, crisp, continuous patter from somewhere in the heart of that crawling bank. The cloud was within fifty yards of where we lay, and we glared at it, all three, uncertain what horror was about to break from the heart of it. I was at Holmes's elbow, and I glanced for an instant at his face. It was pale and exultant, his eyes shining brightly in the moonlight. But suddenly they started forward in a rigid, fixed stare, and his lips parted in amazement. At the same instant Lestrade gave a yell of terror and threw himself face downward upon the ground. I sprang to my feet, my inert hand grasping my pistol, my mind paralyzed by the dreadful shape which had sprung out upon us from the shadows of the fog. A hound it was, an enormous coal-black hound, but not such a hound as mortal eyes have ever seen. Fire burst from its open mouth, its eyes glowed with a smouldering glare, its muzzle and hackles and dewlap were outlined in flickering flame. Never in the delirious dream of a disordered brain could anything more savage, more appalling, more hellish be conceived than that dark form and savage face which broke upon us out of the wall of fog.

Above: Times New Roman (left) and Univers are both highly legible typefaces, but one might argue that Times New Roman (a serif font) works slightly better than the sans serif Univers at this small point size. It was, after all, designed for use in a newspaper.

Many designers don't fully agree with either viewpoint because they're too general; there are lots of equally legible serif and sans serif typefaces – think of Times New Roman versus Univers, for example. The illustration shown here provides a good example of how serif details can enhance the legibility of similar characters.

READABILITY

Reading any text shouldn't require any extra effort from the viewer beyond being able to actually read; words and sentences should be immediately comprehensible because the shapes of regular words become familiar to us over time. We don't tend to read individual words; we read using saccadic movements, which means we take in familiar groups of words using rapid eye movements.

This is where your own design skills come into play, because the responsibility for good readability falls to the designer. The challenge is to ensure that the words, sentences and paragraphs are arranged so those groups of words are given their best chance to jump out of the page into your consciousness.

There was a thin, crisp, continuous patter from somewhere in the heart of that crawling bank. The cloud was within fifty yards of where we lay, and we glared at it, all three, uncertain what horror was about to break from the heart of it. I was at Holmes's elbow, and I glanced for an instant at his face. It was pale and exultant, his eyes shining brightly in the moonlight. But suddenly they started forward in a rigid, fixed stare, and his lips parted in amazement. At the same instant Lestrade gave a yell of terror and threw himself face downward upon the ground. I sprang to my feet, my inert hand grasping my pistol, my mind paralyzed by the dreadful shape which had sprung out upon us from the shadows of the fog. A hound it was, an enormous coal-black hound, but not such a hound as mortal eyes have ever seen.

Above: The formal script Shelley is a well-designed Formal Script typeface, but it doesn't work for lengthy passages of text because readability is compromised.

Think About Intended Use

Achieving a high level of readability doesn't necessarily require the presence of a highly legible font, although it will, of course, help. The commonest mistake is once again inappropriate typeface choice. Some typefaces are designed specifically for text setting, some for large display setting and signage, and so on.

Take some time to find out the background of a typeface's design before using it for a project – most online retailers provide information about any one font's intended use – and always remember that a typeface that is legible when used at large point sizes on a poster isn't necessarily going to work as well when set at smaller point sizes. Using the wrong kind of font doesn't indicate a bad typeface design; it indicates a bad typeface choice.

Character-Count-Per-Line

Apart from that, the other dominant factor affecting readability is character-count-per-line. Including spaces, an ideal count is reckoned to be somewhere between 50 and 75. If a measure (the length of a line of text) becomes too long, the reader's eyes struggle to locate the start of the next line in a paragraph. If it's too short, the reading experience becomes too jerky and loses rhythm. So, for example, novels require a relaxed rhythm, so the measure can and should be at the longer end of the accepted range, while newspaper columns can be set over a shorter measure because the text is generally broken up into shorter snippets of information.

There was a thin, crisp, continuous patter from somewhere in the heart of that crawling bank. The cloud was within fifty yards of where we lay, and we glared at it, all three, uncertain what horror was about to break from the heart of it. I was at Holmes's elbow, and I glanced for an instant at his face. It was pale and exultant, his eyes shining brightly in the moonlight. But suddenly they started forward in a rigid, fixed stare, and his lips parted in amazement. At the same instant Lestrade gave a yell of terror and threw himself face downward upon the ground. I sprang to my feet, my inert hand grasping my pistol, my mind paralyzed by the dreadful shape which had sprung out upon us from the shadows of the fog. A hound it was, an enormous coal-black hound, but not such a hound as mortal eyes have ever seen. Fire burst from its open mouth, its eyes glowed with a smouldering glare, its muzzle and hackles and dewlap were outlined in flickering flame. Never in the delirious dream of a disordered brain could anything more savage, more appalling, more hellish be conceived than that dark form and savage face which broke upon us out of the wall of fog.

There was a thin, crisp, continuous patter from somewhere in the heart of that crawling bank. The cloud was within fifty yards of where we lay, and we glared at it, all three, uncertain what horror was about to break from the heart of it. I was at Holmes's elbow, and I glanced for an instant at his face. It was pale and exultant, his eyes shining brightly in the moonlight. But suddenly they started forward in a rigid, fixed stare, and his lips parted in amazement. At the same instant Lestrade gave a yell of terror and threw himself face downward upon the ground. I sprang to my feet, my inert hand grasping my pistol, my mind paralyzed by the dreadful shape which had sprung out upon us from the shadows of the fog. A hound it was, an enormous coal-black hound, but not such a hound as mortal eyes have ever seen. Fire burst from its open mouth, its eyes glowed with a smouldering glare, its muzzle and hackles and dewlap were outlined in flickering flame. Never in the delirious dream of a disordered brain could anything more savage, more appalling, more hellish be conceived than that dark form and savage face which broke upon us out of the wall of fog.

Above: At just over 50 characters per line, the first text sample (set in Sabon) scans comfortably from line to line. Over a wider measure of around 120 characters, it becomes much harder to locate the start of each subsequent line, creating bad readability.

UPPERCASE AND LOWERCASE

Have you ever wondered why characters are referred to as uppercase and lowercase? The terms originate from the days when type was set by hand using individual metal characters, known as sorts.

SORTING THE CHARACTERS

To help the compositors locate each character, sorts were organized in special drawers, with a standardized layout of compartments in various different sizes. The compartments for the frequently used characters, such as vowels, were larger so they could hold more sorts, while the smallest compartments were reserved for consonants such as 'j', 'q' or 'z'. Crucially, the capitals were stored in one drawer at the top of the font cabinet, and the small letters in another below, hence you have the uppercase and the lowercase.

Below: Before mechanized typesetting was introduced, individual 'sorts' were composed by hand, with the compositor selecting from either the upper or lower case.

There was a thin, crisp, continuous patter from somewhere in the heart of that crawling bank. The cloud was within fifty yards of where we lay, and we glared at it, all three, uncertain what horror was about to break from the heart of it. I was at Holmes's elbow, and I glanced for an instant at his face. It was pale and exultant, his eyes shining brightly in the moonlight. But suddenly they started forward in a rigid, fixed stare, and his lips parted in amazement. At the same instant Lestrade gave a yell of terror and threw himself face downward upon the ground. I sprang to my feet, my inert hand grasping my pistol, my mind paralyzed by the dreadful shape which had sprung out upon us from the shadows of the fog. A hound it was, an enormous coal-black hound, but not such a hound as mortal eyes have ever seen.

Above/Right: Imagine trying to read the whole of *The Hound of the Baskervilles* set in capital letters. It would be very hard work.

THERE WAS A THIN, CRISP, CONTINUOUS PATTER FROM SOMEWHERE IN THE HEART OF THAT CRAWLING BANK. THE CLOUD WAS WITHIN FIFTY YARDS OF WHERE WE LAY, AND WE GLARED AT IT, ALL THREE, UNCERTAIN WHAT HORROR WAS ABOUT TO BREAK FROM THE HEART OF IT. I WAS AT HOLMES'S ELBOW, AND I GLANCED FOR AN INSTANT AT HIS FACE. IT WAS PALE AND EXULTANT, HIS EYES SHINING BRIGHTLY IN THE MOONLIGHT. BUT SUDDENLY THEY STARTED FORWARD IN A RIGID, FIXED STARE, AND HIS LIPS PARTED IN AMAZEMENT. AT THE SAME INSTANT LESTRADE GAVE A YELL OF TERROR AND THREW HIMSELF FACE DOWNWARD UPON THE GROUND. I SPRANG TO MY FEET, MY INERT HAND GRASPING MY PISTOL, MY MIND PARALYZED BY THE DREADFUL SHAPE WHICH HAD SPRUNG OUT UPON US FROM THE SHADOWS OF THE FOG.

Use Them Both

There's a close link between the use of uppercase and lowercase setting and our previous topic of legibility and readability. We tend to always set running text using the standard combination of uppercase and lowercase characters, and there are a couple of very sound reasons for doing that. Firstly, reading long passages of text set entirely in uppercase (or caps) is not particularly easy on the eye, so it is not recommended. All-cap setting is the typographic equivalent of shouting at your readers and nobody wants to be shouted at. Secondly, and perhaps more crucially, readability is adversely affected, because words set entirely in uppercase lack a unique shape.

THE WORD SUPERIORITY EFFECT

Way back in 1886, the eminent American psychologist James McKeen Cattell put forward a theory about the way we read words. During monitored tests, he was able to demonstrate that, after very short exposure times and at a close reading distance, subjects were more likely to identify and recall individual words than they were single letters. This is known as the Word Superiority Effect, and the theory, although it's been challenged over the years, still holds water. It all sounds rather scientific and not very typographic, but it is relevant.

Above: James McKeen Cattell's 1886 test was the first to put forward the theory that readers were able to recognize individual words more quickly than individual letters.

A Word Image Bank

The Word Superiority Effect relies on the brain's ability to recall images that it has stored in a kind of word image bank. A good analogy is a computer caching frequently referenced information, so it can recall it quickly without having to search its entire hard drive every time it processes a piece of data. Adult readers build up a massive database of word shapes, which enables them to read more quickly, but this only works effectively for words set in a combination of upper- and lowercase. Words set in uppercase have no shape; they're simply rectangular blocks, so we have to visually decipher each word as we read, slowing us down. We're talking about fractions of a second, of course, but it all adds up when you're reading long passages of text.

OTHER OPTIONS

Does this mean that lowercase characters are more legible? No, because all-cap headlines set in the right choice of font are highly legible too. It's simply a case of using the right tool for the job in order to maximize readability and create visually pleasing typography.

But what has this to do with typeface choice? Less than it has to do with font use, because most fonts contain the full character set of upper- and lowercase characters, but this isn't always the case. For example, the extremely popular Trajan from Adobe features small caps instead of lowercase. Setting running text with small caps can work very well because it provides a different kind of emphasis to the text, falling somewhere between all-caps and mixed-case setting, but it shouldn't be overdone or the emphasis is lost.

Right: Setting text using small caps in a typeface such as Trajan provides a kind of middle-ground, where readability is retained but emphasis is heightened.

Preface

*A **Chancery judge** once* had the kindness to inform me, as one of a company of some hundred and fifty men and women not labouring under any suspicions of lunacy, that the Court of Chancery, though the shining subject of much popular prejudice (at which point I thought the judge's eye had a cast in my direction), was almost immaculate. There had been, he admitted, a trivial blemish or so in its rate of progress, but this was exaggerated and had been entirely owing to the "parsimony of the public," which guilty public, it appeared, had been until lately bent in the most determined manner on by no means enlarging the number of Chancery judges appointed—I believe by Richard the Second, but any other king will do as well.

This seemed to me too profound a joke to be inserted in the body of this book or I should have restored it to Conversation Kenge or to Mr. Vholes, with one or other of whom I think it must have originated. In such mouths I might have coupled it with an apt quotation from one of Shakespeare's sonnets:

"My nature is subdued
To what it works in, like the dyer's hand:
Pity me, then, and wish I were renewed!"

But as it is wholesome that the parsimonious public should know what has been doing, and still is doing, in this connexion, I mention here that everything set forth in these pages concerning the Court of Chancery is substantially true, and within the truth. The case of Gridley is in no essential altered from one of actual occurrence, made public by a disinterested person who was professionally acquainted with the whole of the monstrous wrong from beginning to end. At the present moment (August, 1853) there is a suit before the court which was commenced nearly twenty years ago, in which from thirty to forty counsel have been known to appear at one time, in which costs have been incurred to the amount of seventy thousand pounds, which is *A Friendly Suit*, and which is (I am assured) no nearer to its termination now than when it was begun. There is another well-known suit in Chancery, not yet decided, which was commenced before the close of the last century and in which more than double the amount of seventy thousand pounds has been swallowed up in costs. If I wanted other authorities for Jarndyce and Jarndyce, I could rain them on these pages, to the shame of—a parsimonious public.

There is only one other point on which I offer a word of remark. The possibility of what is called spontaneous combustion has been denied since the death of Mr. Krook, and my

11

Above: The brain finds it quicker and easier to recognize word shapes rather than to decipher individual letters.

THERE WAS A THIN, CRISP, CONTINUOUS PATTER FROM SOMEWHERE IN THE HEART OF THAT CRAWLING BANK. THE CLOUD WAS WITHIN FIFTY YARDS OF WHERE WE LAY, AND WE GLARED AT IT, ALL THREE, UNCERTAIN WHAT HORROR WAS ABOUT TO BREAK FROM THE HEART OF IT. I WAS AT HOLMES'S ELBOW, AND I GLANCED FOR AN INSTANT AT HIS FACE. IT WAS PALE AND EXULTANT, HIS EYES SHINING BRIGHTLY IN THE MOONLIGHT. BUT SUDDENLY THEY STARTED FORWARD IN A RIGID, FIXED STARE, AND HIS LIPS PARTED IN AMAZEMENT. AT THE SAME INSTANT LESTRADE GAVE A YELL OF TERROR AND

TYPOGRAPHIC CONTRAST

Typographic contrast has a couple of meanings. The term can be used to describe how different areas of a layout work together to create a hierarchy, where important sections of the text stand out; or it can describe the difference between the thickest and thinnest strokes that make up any one character of a font.

HOW TO ALTER CONTRAST

Let's look at the ways typeface choice can affect a layout's contrast.

Brioso Light
Brioso Regular
Brioso Medium
Brioso Semibold
Brioso Bold

Above: The delightful typeface Brioso from Adobe includes five separate weights that can be used to create differing levels of typographic contrast.

Weight Variation

Firstly, weight variation is one of the simplest ways to introduce contrast. Larger typeface families include a broad range of weights, from light to bold or perhaps black for heavier setting. Remember that the heaviest weights of a family don't often make good choices for long passages of running text, because readability can be adversely affected.

Above: Bodoni (on the left) is a high-contrast typeface as the widths of the strokes vary considerably. News Gothic, on the other hand, displays minimal contrast.

Form

Secondly, form plays its part. Form describes the shape of a typeface's letterforms, and wide letterforms with large counters (*see* 'The Anatomy of Type' on page 56–57), open apertures and minimal contrast in the letterforms themselves create a light overall contrast within a layout. Serif faces are particularly well suited for lightly textured setting, because the serifs generate a little more white space between characters than the average sans serif. At the opposite end of the scale, contrasty letterforms, typefaces with heavy monolinear strokes, or those with a narrow character width creating smaller counters, create a dark texture.

TYPOGRAPHIC COLOUR

The phrase 'typographic colour' doesn't actually refer to type that has a colour other than black applied to it. In type terms, the meaning is more closely related to the tonal value – or, if you like, the visual weight – of a block of text.

GETTING THE COLOUR RIGHT

In order to gauge the level of typographic colour, one should stare at a layout (a printed copy works best) and squint so the type becomes blurred. The resulting grey tone that you should now be able to see in place of the sharp text is the typographic colour.

There are reasons you may want to achieve a particular level of typographic colour. Perhaps your text needs to be stern or impactful and express a dark colour, or light and airy, where a lighter colour would be more appropriate. It's all about the mood you want to achieve. The exact colour you require can be fine-tuned very precisely through typeface choice.

Typefaces and Colour

Typefaces that display a high level of contrast can provide a greater degree of colour, but only if the thinnest strokes are not too thin. For example, a Modern typeface, such as Bodoni, won't necessarily colour dark, especially if a lighter weight of the typeface is being used. Sans serif typefaces with uniformly heavy strokes are a good choice for a darker overall colour for your text setting. If a lighter colour is needed, low contrast serifs work well, as do lightly flowing script typefaces.

There was a thin, crisp, continuous patter from somewhere in the heart of that crawling bank. The cloud was within fifty yards of where we lay, and we glared at it, all three, uncertain what horror was about to break from the heart of it. I was at Holmes's elbow, and I glanced for an instant at his face. It was pale and exultant, his eyes shining brightly in the moonlight. But suddenly they started forward in a rigid, fixed stare, and his lips parted in amazement.

At the same instant Lestrade gave a yell of terror and threw himself face downward upon the ground. I sprang to my feet, my inert hand grasping my pistol, my mind paralyzed by the dreadful shape which had sprung out upon us from the shadows of the fog. A hound it was, an enormous coal-black hound, but not such a hound as mortal eyes have ever seen. Fire burst from its open mouth, its eyes glowed with a smouldering glare, its muzzle and hackles and dewlap were outlined in flickering flame. Never in the delirious dream of a disordered brain could anything more savage, more appalling, more hellish be conceived than that dark form and savage face which broke upon us out of the wall of fog.

Above: In the first paragraph, the narrow letterforms and minimal contrast of Trade Gothic colours darkly, while the open apertures and relatively low x-height of Arno look much lighter.

TIGHT OR OPEN SPACING?

Letterspacing affects colour significantly; if you use tight spacing and a condensed font, the colour is on the darker side, while open spacing and a font with relatively wide character widths pushes the colour towards the lighter end of the scale. Lowercase text setting always appears slightly lighter overall in colour, because of the greater variation of forms.

There was a thin, crisp, continuous patter from somewhere in the heart of that crawling bank. The cloud was within fifty yards of where we lay, and we glared at it, all three, uncertain what horror was about to break from the heart of it. I was at Holmes's elbow, and I glanced for an instant at his face. It was pale and exultant, his eyes shining brightly in the moonlight. But suddenly they started forward in a rigid, fixed stare, and his lips parted in amazement.

At the same instant Lestrade gave a yell of terror and threw himself face downward upon the ground. I sprang to my feet, my inert hand grasping my pistol, my mind paralyzed by the dreadful shape which had sprung out upon us from the shadows of the fog. A hound it was, an enormous coal-black hound, but not such a hound as mortal eyes have ever seen. Fire burst from its open mouth, its eyes glowed with a smouldering glare, its muzzle and hackles and dewlap were outlined in flickering flame. Never in the delirious dream of a disordered brain could anything more savage, more appalling, more hellish be conceived than that dark form

Drawn to Darkness

Always remember that the eye is drawn towards darker areas of a layout, to create a natural hierarchy (or typographic contrast). Designers often set an introductory paragraph of a layout in a heavier weight of the chosen typeface (as on the opposite page), or perhaps use an alternative complementary font that boosts the colour even more.

LEFT: Both paragraphs are set in the same point size and weight of Trade Gothic, but the (rather exaggerated) open spacing of the first paragraph produces a much lighter typographic colour.

CONVEYING CONTENT

The title of this section may sound obvious – why would anyone attempt to put together a typographic design concept without trying to convey the content? Isn't that the whole idea behind graphic design – or graphic communication, as it's also called?

THE FAVOURED FEW

Surprisingly, many graphic design projects are brought crashing down simply because typeface choices aren't thought through carefully enough. I can't tell you what my favourite typeface is because I don't have a particular favourite. There are too many great ones to choose from

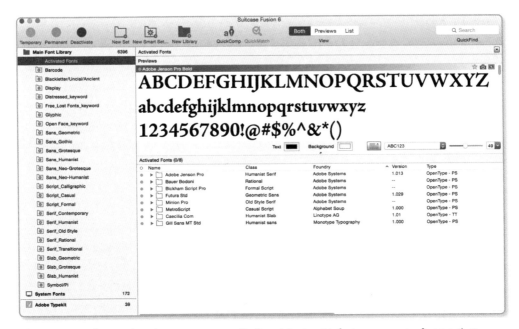

Above: As your collection of typefaces grows, you may find it useful to invest in font management software such as Suitcase Fusion from Extensis. It'll allow you to browse fonts visually and to organize them into folders based on classification.

and I would place a hefty bet that many other designers would give the same response. What most seasoned designers will have is a collection of favoured typefaces which they've purchased for use in different contexts, but, of course, those typefaces won't necessarily be your favourites too.

SUBJECTIVE VERSUS OBJECTIVE

It can't be emphasized enough that typeface choice is not and never can be an entirely objective process. There's no single font that's perfect for any one specific project. The process of choosing a typeface is by its very nature a subjective one, and sometimes the best option is reached by following your gut feeling. However, one can build a degree of objectivity into the process by considering whether or not a typeface manages to convey the content correctly and effectively.

Don't Overdo It

Unfortunately, some folk do appear to have a couple of favourites, perhaps one serif and one sans serif, and feel that it's perfectly fine to use them for absolutely everything. This is like the stopped clock that tells the correct time only twice a day; always using the same typeface might work well every now and again, but not always. Even when it's the right choice, if you haven't thought things through properly, how will you know? With a little knowledge, combining type history, type style and classification, and your own instincts, you can make confident and assured choices that work with, rather than against, your projects.

MAKING THE RIGHT CHOICE

Wedding invites are one of the projects undertaken by as many amateur designers as there are professional commissions. It is lovely to design your own wedding invitation – it keeps things very personal and saves money, which can be put towards more champagne for the reception. But why do most people go with a formal script typeface? The answer is it's the default choice, and professionals as well as amateurs are guilty of taking the easy route by saying, 'Yes, Palace Script will look perfect.' It's not wrong to use a formal script, just a little predictable.

Be Creative

Lazy typeface choices aren't exclusive to wedding invites, but they are a good example of the kind of project that can potentially be made a lot more interesting by conveying the content with a more creative typeface choice, which lifts the project visually.

The following pointers may help you think outside the typeface box:

- **Use typefaces to complement**: The couple in question may be into the 1950s and drive a retro car, so a cool 1950s typeface, such as Melior, designed by the great Hermann Zapf in 1952, or a contemporary reworking of a casual script, such as House Casual, from digital foundry House Industries, would complement the big day.

Mr and Mrs Smith
would like to invite
James & Sarah
to the wedding of their daughter
Susan
and Malcolm Jones
on Saturday 27th June
at
All Saints Church
Service at 3pm
RSVP: mrs.smith@gmail.com

Mr & Mrs Smith
would like to invite
James & Sarah
to the wedding of their daughter
Susan Smith
and Malcolm Jones
on **Saturday 27th June**
at
All Saints Church
Service at 3pm
RSVP: mrs.smith@gmail.com

Above: In this very simple example, the use of Bauer Bodoni feels no less elegant than a default Formal script. Furthermore, improved legibility means point sizes and weights can be more varied, providing typographic texture.

○ **Use typefaces to reflect**: The couple might be into heavy metal music, so why not go for a Blackletter, such as Fette Fraktur? Perhaps that's going a little too far, but you get the idea.

○ **Use something different**: You don't have to stick to the style of typeface that most other people plump for to convey content purposefully. Every project has its own unique blend of influences, and it is important to evaluate each one as a whole and map that on to your typeface choice, to help achieve a standout result that wows your client.

THE LATEST TREND

Designers are naturally susceptible to being wooed by the latest cool typefaces to be released. It's all too easy to spot a great new typeface on a website or in a foundry's newsletter and decide it's the greatest typeface you've ever seen and that you must use it as soon as possible

Above: The sensuous curves of Lust Script from digital foundry Positype look great, but is it the best choice for an accountancy firm's new logo? Perhaps not, but you never know. Clients can be as unpredictable as font choices!

– in fact, on the very next project you're commissioned to undertake. But will it convey the content accurately? When one is suffering from self-induced font blindness, smitten with the latest offering from Hoefler & Co. or Font Bureau, inappropriate things can happen between designers and their briefs.

Seriously, though, it would be pure luck if a newly released typeface you were desperate to use matched perfectly with your very next project, and if you really love a particular typeface, it's worth waiting for the right project before you use it, otherwise it's a waste.

THINK ABOUT IT

Conveying typographic content with visual accuracy requires a little thought applied from a few different angles. There's the classification of the typeface (see pages 58–61), which indicates its historical influence, giving you a big clue about its appropriateness for a project. You should check out what the typeface was designed to be used for: text, display and signage, novelty headline, and so on. This in itself helps to provide you with further clues about the suitability of your typeface choice. Think about how it will colour on the page, affecting the mood of the layout.

And finally, decide for yourself whether it feels right – if you think it does, there is a good chance you are right.

ORGANIC STRUCTURE

In the Oxford English Dictionary, hierarchy is defined as 'a body of things ranked one above the other, especially with respect to authority or dominance'. Typographic hierarchy is just that, indicating the level of importance given to a headline, passage of text, caption, and so on in a layout.

ACHIEVING A SUCCESSFUL HIERARCHY

Without typographic hierarchy, layouts would look terribly bland and it would be difficult for the reader to navigate around the key information points contained in the text. But how is it achieved? Have a look through this list to see what factors you should take into account:

1. The point size and weight of the chosen font.
2. The position and orientation of the text elements within the layout.

3. On a more subtle level, typographic contrast (*see* page 34) is an important method used to introduce what might be termed a silent hierarchy, where the texture of the type across the whole of the layout draws the eye on a subliminal level to areas that require emphasis.

TOO MANY TYPEFACES

Have you ever looked at a flyer for a club night or a marketing brochure for a sale at your local furniture superstore, and felt as though you were being assaulted by an army of marauding fonts? Very occasionally, using a dozen typefaces within a single layout might work, but only if the nature of the content lends itself to being conveyed in a haphazard way. Club nights and music festivals are often hectic affairs, with lots of things happening at the same time, so for this kind of event, it's possible to pull off a leaflet or poster design that tears around in all sorts

of typographic directions. However, in the majority of cases, it's not a great idea to create hierarchy using lots of different typefaces.

SALE NOW ON!
Everything must go this week!

100% GUARANTEED PRICES

- **Special offers on kitchen units and furniture**
- *All stainless steel sinks half-price*
- *Sofas and armchairs on interest-free credit*
- Buy one sofa get one free
- **Bathroom suites with free shower**
- Free delivery on all items

The sky's the limit on bargain basement day

Above: How many typefaces does one need for any one project? Not many in most cases, or you may end up with a complete mess, as exemplified here.

Keep It Simple

The problem with multiple typefaces used in combination is that they can end up fighting for attention, creating a situation where there is no hierarchy at all. Take the furniture store example – a headline in a bold Slab serif will catch the eye, but if a heavier sans serif appears further down the page, announcing 'Our best deal today on the latest dining suite,' and a sidebar set in a flamboyant script trumpets the merits of stainless steel worktops, the reader will struggle to decide which piece of information is the most important. Limiting the number of typefaces to only those you really need is an exercise in restraint on the part of the designer, and it's a worthy discipline to master.

GETTING YOUR HIERARCHY RIGHT

As a basic guide to getting your hierarchical structure just right, follow the pointers here:

1. First, pick the typeface you want to use for your main running text, deciding on the best point size and the appropriate weight, which will give you your overall typographic colour.

2. Once you have that nailed, work with that typeface for all other choices. For example, for the headline, take the same typeface family and change only one or two attributes; perhaps increase the point size or go up a weight, but try not to go overboard with a wildly different typeface style in a much bolder weight, set entirely in uppercase. That last sentence isn't a hard and fast rule; it's not wrong to mix typefaces that are very different, but creating good hierarchy with a limited range of typeface styles generally focuses the reader on the information rather than the design, which is a common goal for all good typography.

Headline

Introduction

Text

Caption

Above: A simple hierarchy mixing the sans serif font News Gothic with the serif font Palatino provides ample distinction between typographic elements.

Quick Tip

Mixing two serif typefaces prominently in a single layout is often a bad move, akin to wearing a Hawaiian shirt with checked trousers. They simply don't belong together, and people in the know will stare.

3. If you do want to use complementary typefaces, think about mixing a good hard-working sans serif, such as News Gothic, with a classically proportioned serif, such as Palatino. Typefaces with the overall attributes that these two examples possess generally combine well and create good hierarchy.

HIERARCHY THROUGH TEXTURE

As we mentioned, fonts from different typeface families don't always work well together when combined, but that doesn't mean it's a no-go area. As long as you're careful to ensure that dominant typeface styles don't completely overpower other typographic elements, typographic texture can be used to create another form of hierarchy in a layout, which relies on colour or texture.

Typography Exhibition
A RETROSPECTIVE FROM LETTERPRESS TO OPENTYPE

European typeface design and its influence on poster design in the Americas

How Caslon and Baskerville moulded the visual and culutral sensibilities of the American public during the earliest days of colonialism and its lasting effect on graphic design today.

October 12 – November 6

Above: There are only two typefaces used in this graphic for an imaginary exhibition, both of which were designed some 130 years apart. However, the combination works perfectly well and creates an overall typographic texture.

Inspiration from Others

Experienced designers will approach these kinds of choices intuitively. They'll remember typeface combinations that worked well previously and come back to them for the right kinds of project. Once again, these will be personal picks, so may not be everyone's cup of tea, but looking at what other designers have brought together is always a reasonable place to start when mulling over your own choices.

There are a few ground rules that you can apply here too. Historical links based on type classifications (see pages 58–61) are really useful for creating harmonious font pairings, and a comparison of the similarities between the proportions of a font's characters will contribute to your decision-making process.

Don't Go Overboard

But remember – always stick to the basic idea of not taking things too far. Many projects teeter precariously on the edge of having one too many elements, and it's those designers who go just far enough, but know when to stop, who are often the most successful.

CONVEYING INTENT

Faced with a design brief that involves incorporating text that covers a specific subject area, a designer would read as much of the text as possible (or necessary) to understand the intent of the information within it. When it comes to subjects that are either historical or cultural, content is one of the major influencers of typeface choice.

DON'T DIVE STRAIGHT IN ...

It's surprising how many designers do not read the text but simply dive in with whatever fonts they're keen to use, because they like the look of them. It's true that not everyone can afford to purchase new typefaces for every project when they don't already own the perfect choice, but that's no excuse for taking a pot-shot at whatever alternative typeface might work.

... Read the Text First

If you really want to understand what a passage of text is trying to convey, it's rarely sufficient to read the crossheads and a few lines of the first paragraph. Sure, if you're lucky, a synopsis might be provided as part of the design brief, which summarizes everything neatly and explains exactly what visual message your client wishes to convey. But it's still better to read some of the text before leaping in with suggestions for typeface choice or typographic styling. It's here that your knowledge of the historical origins of type styles and how they've influenced contemporary typeface design comes into play.

Make Informed Choices

Perhaps there may be boxed call-outs throughout the text, which provide perfect jumping-off points for your design decisions, or maybe a run-through of the captions for an illustrated book or brochure will give you what you need. Either way, do your homework first and apply what you find to your decision.

DO SOME RESEARCH

Here's an example. You've been asked to design a brochure to accompany an exhibition featuring paintings and sculpture from the Renaissance period. What typefaces will you use? First of all, you need to check what years are covered by the Renaissance, so a quick online search will tell you that it could be anywhere from the late-fourteenth to the seventeenth century. However, the text indicates clearly that the exhibition is about the French Renaissance, a period that began a little later than the original movement, which centred around the Italian region of Tuscany and the city of Florence.

Renaissance
Renaissance
Renaissance

Above: Any one of these typefaces could work for a project about the Renaissance, but there are subtle differences between Jenson, Bembo and Garamond which tie them to either the fifteenth or sixteenth centuries.

Right Time, Right Font

The Italian Renaissance arrived in France in 1495, which is, coincidentally, the year that Francesco Griffo first cut the font that would eventually become Bembo. So perhaps you could use Bembo for your text face. It's a lovely design and would certainly look great, but perhaps there's a better option ... Just a few decades later, in Paris, Claude Garamond cut his eponymous fonts, making them the first and the most important typefaces of the French Renaissance. What better choice could there be? There are lots of very good digital versions of Garamond to choose from, which are also inexpensive.

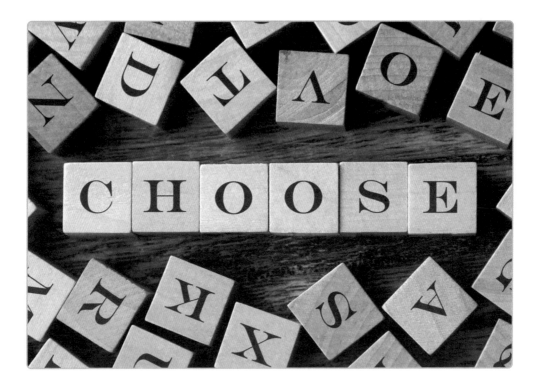

Getting the Context Right

That's a relatively simple example, which involved very little deduction, but hopefully it indicates how the simple process of reading and research can point you to a highly contextual typeface choice, which will truly convey the essence of the textual content. There are plenty of helpful books and websites (some of which are listed at the end of this book) that will aid your research, but remember – if you don't read the text, you'll never fully grasp the intent.

1900s	**Eckmann**
1910s	Plantin
1920s	Futura
1930s	Peignot
1940s	**Figaro**
1950s	Melior
1960s	Americana
1970s	ITC Benguiat
1980s	Rotis Semi Serif
1990s	Template Gothic

Above: Take a look at the way typeface design developed throughout the twentieth century, in line with other visual culture, and you'll get a sense of how to represent each decade typographically.

FONT VERSUS TYPEFACE

The first thing to clear up here is that the difference between font and typeface isn't such a big deal as it used to be. Typographers used to get quite sniffy about the distinction, but nowadays the terms are relatively interchangeable. However, it's still useful to think of the words as having different meanings in typographic terms.

WHICH IS WHICH?

Broadly speaking, a font is what you use when setting type, and a typeface is what you see when you look at type. Further to this, a font can be thought of as a component of a larger

{
Baskerville Regular
Baskerville Regular Italic
Baskerville Semibold
Baskerville Semibold Italic
Baskerville Bold
Baskerville Bold Italic
}

Above: Baskerville is a typeface, or more precisely a typeface family, but Baskerville Bold Italic is a font.

typeface family, and this is where the older distinction narrows. You can now elevate a font to the status of a typeface, largely because of modern technological advances.

Font Families

In the days of metal type, a font was defined as the character set of a typeface in a particular point size and a particular weight. For example, Baskerville is the name of a typeface, but 12-point Baskerville Bold Italic is a font within that family.

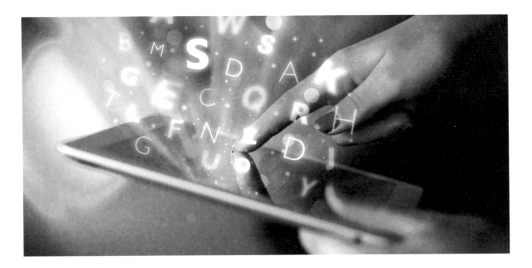

OpenType

This remained true for many years and transcended the phototypesetting technology of the 1970s and 1980s, with the earliest formats of digital PostScript screen fonts assigned specific points sizes, usually 10-, 12- and 24-point. Other sizes were scaled from these screen fonts using a separate printer font file. Now, the OpenType format is far more advanced, and one file contains all the information for all the point sizes of a weight.

It is also largely a generational thing. Non-designers and younger professional designers are probably more likely to use 'font' as a default, while older designers are likely to favour the word 'typeface'.

THE ANATOMY OF TYPE

The names assigned to the various parts of a typeface's letterforms can vary from source to source, but the labels assigned here are generally accepted as the most common terms in use today by the majority of designers and typographers.

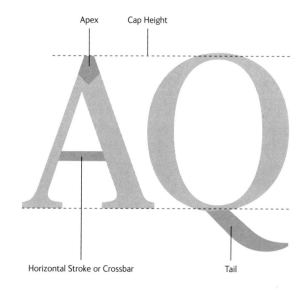

Apex   Cap Height

Horizontal Stroke or Crossbar   Tail

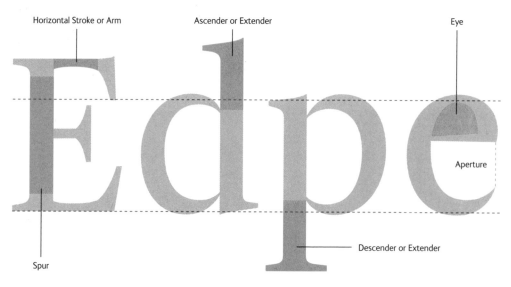

Horizontal Stroke or Arm   Ascender or Extender   Eye

Aperture

Spur   Descender or Extender

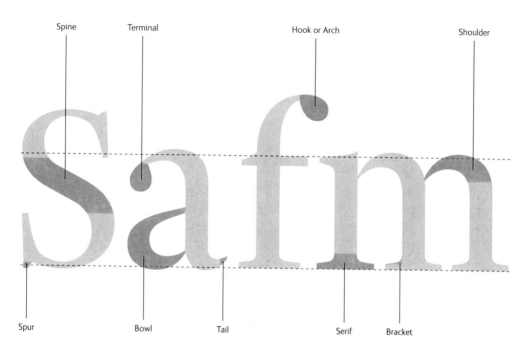

Spine   Terminal   Hook or Arch   Shoulder

Spur   Bowl   Tail   Serif   Bracket

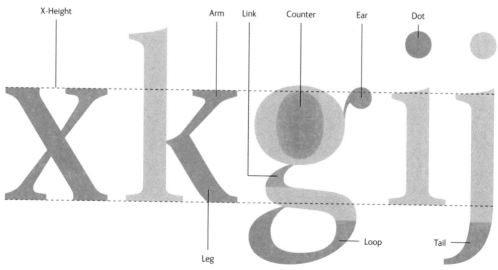

X-Height   Arm   Link   Counter   Ear   Dot

Leg   Loop   Tail

TYPE CLASSIFICATION

Type classification is challenging. Some typefaces fall very obviously into a particular slot, but there are many that have characteristics that could place them in more than one class. This makes it difficult to establish a definitive system for type classification – but that hasn't stopped various individuals from trying during the last hundred years or so.

VOX-ATYPI

The best-known system, which for years held sway as the most definitive yet, is the Vox-ATypI, devised by the French historian Maximilien Vox in 1954, and it's still in general use today. It works pretty well, but is increasingly challenged by many energetic new typeface designs, because they've been designed to respond to a whole new set of demands. Principal among these is the need for type to function well both in print and onscreen.

Below: Maximilien Vox devised his system for type classification in 1954 and it remains in use today as a basis for more advanced systems which include additional contemporary categories.

The system is based on chronological style and provides a good jumping-off point for choosing and combining typefaces. If you build up a decent general knowledge of all the various tell-tale characteristics associated with each class, you'll be able to use that knowledge to pick appropriate faces for your projects, and you will be able to pair up typefaces more effectively when several different font styles are used.

A NEW SYSTEM

The system laid out below is a slightly different version of Vox-ATypI, with some minor adjustments. You can read more about it in Stephen Coles' book *The Anatomy of Type* (or *Geometry of Type* for some editions). It introduces a Rational serif category, helping to clear up a grey area that exists around the period covering the late-eighteenth century and the influences it still exerts over contemporary typeface design. Hopefully, it will help to explain further why some typefaces work well in certain contexts, and why some look good in combination while others do not.

THE CLASSIFICATIONS

- **Ancient**: Any typeface designs that existed before the fifteenth century. These were mainly Blackletter, based closely on existing handwriting styles popular in Central Europe during the medieval period.

Above: Ancient

Above: Humanist serif

- **Humanist serif**: These are also referred to as Venetian serifs on occasion, and are roman letterforms with a calligraphic feel, which makes them look as though they could have been drawn with a broad-nibbed pen. This style dates from the mid-fifteenth century onwards.

Above: Old Style serif

- **Old Style serif**: A close relation to its predecessor, Old Style still retains the calligraphic element but with a less organic feel to the strokes and serifs, and dates from the late-fifteenth century onwards.

- **Transitional serif**: Dating from the mid-eighteenth century onwards, Transitionals are far less calligraphic, with letterforms that appear more upright.

Baskerville

Left:
Transitional serif

- **Rational serif**: Dating from the late-eighteenth century, Rationals include Moderns, and commonly feature a lot of contrast in the thickness and thinness of the stems. Letterforms appear to be more constructed than drawn.

Walbaum

Left:
Rational serif

- **Script**: Any typeface from the late-eighteenth century onwards that attempts to emulate the look of handwritten text or elegant calligraphy.

Left:
Script

- **Slab serif**: Faces from the early-nineteenth century onwards, which feature heavy serifs similar in width to the stems.

Clarendon

Left:
Slab serif

○ **Sans serif**: These typefaces have simpler letterforms, which lack serifs, and date from the early-nineteenth century, but are more prolifically a twentieth-century style.

Gill Sans

Left: Sans serif

○ **Contemporary serif**: A relatively new classification, which exists to catch any serif typefaces that can't be placed directly into any earlier category.

Neue Swift

Left: Contemporary serif

THE BASICS

SERIF OR SANS SERIF?

Chapter 2's 'The Anatomy of Type', on pages 56–61, describes the two overarching categories of fonts: serif typefaces and sans serif typefaces. These two physical distinctions have come to represent two different typographic voices, as well as much debate on which is the most legible.

TONE

Which should you choose? Your answer is in the text and with the reader. Given the tone of the text, ask yourself, what suits it best? Serif typefaces, such as Garamond, are used most often. Their serifs provide a formal flourish, lending themselves to being considered classic or traditional, elegant and conventional. Sans serif typefaces, with their simplified, geometric

Below: The Garamond serif typeface, seen here on the left, is more commonly used in text than the more design-orientated Helvetica (right).

shapes and strokes of uniform weights, are associated with modernity and contemporary design. Helvetica, designed in the 1950s, is perhaps the most famous.

Read the text and decide what tone needs to be achieved. An instruction manual with short spurts of text, lists and tables may call for the direct clarity of a sans serif typeface. Conversely, a nineteenth-century novel would most likely read with most integrity in a serif typeface familiar to the Victorians.

Exceptions

Both categories defy convention often enough to speak beyond their associations. Typefaces such as Gill Sans took on a more human nature by showing what were almost perfectly straight lines, subtle undulations and tapers, resulting in friendly sans serifs. There are serif typefaces that are modern and fresh, and there are sans serif faces that take cues from the handmade origins of typeface design.

Below: The Gill Sans typeface is a friendly font, giving straight lines slight curves.

MEDIUM

After determining the tone, consider the medium by which it will be read. Whether to select a serif or a sans serif for the reading of body text has been a big debate within the graphic design industry for decades. The which-is-better argument continues chiefly because there have been no conclusive studies measuring which one we find more legible. For this reason, opinions continue to be based on subjective observation and, perhaps most often, personal taste.

SERIF OR SANS FOR PRINT?

Are fonts with serifs best suited for reading printed text? Are they more legible? Purists hold unwaveringly to the belief that they are. It could be because the serifs themselves create visual links – small black bridges – between the letterforms, visually connecting the letters horizontally, keeping the words intact. But a more compelling argument favouring serif typefaces for body text is based on the design of the letterforms themselves.

As covered in Chapter 2, the strokes of serif fonts have thicks and thins, which make letterforms distinct from each other, so recognizing words is made easier. Conversely, a sans serif typeface is typically built from uniform strokes, making beautifully simple forms, but supposedly requiring more effort on the part of the reader to decipher the difference between letters and words. For all the seemingly convincing arguments for and against, until formal work has been done to confirm exactly how our eyes scan text, we can focus on selecting typefaces that reflect the text best.

Now is a good time to introduce a sans serif font designed with reading body text in mind. By appropriating some of the organic calligraphic qualities inherent in serifs, typefaces such as Optima are highly legible and are reliable options for both display and body text.

Above: The highly legible Optima typeface is reliable for clear display of text.

SERIF OR SANS FOR SCREENS

One area less disputed is the use of sans serif fonts for onscreen reading. It is true that our screens are becoming clearer and clearer as technological developments speed forward, but they still cannot match the clarity of ink on paper. The earliest screen resolutions were low, and because letterforms were redesigned out of 0s and 1s, there was little place for the fine lines of serifs. As screens increased in quality, so did the fonts, but sans serifs remained the most direct and clear choice. Designing fonts for onscreen use is now a major component of a type designer's career. Chapter 4 will elaborate, and Chapter 9 lists some good typefaces for website and app design.

SERIF OR SANS FOR DISPLAY

Just as things could go either way for body text, so it is for display text. A large, bold sans serif certainly achieves the readability needs of today's major headlines, and is most commonly used. But a large serif typeface can be an equally compelling, eye-catching solution, and should not be dismissed.

Exhibition
World's Fair
GARDEN PAVILLION
Grand Palais

Above: The classic and very popular Rockwell font is most commonly used for headlines, signage, and logos.

Is there something else that might work? Consider a slab serif typeface for display text. Slab serifs have formal shapes, keeping them highly legible, and their amplified serifs provide more visual interest. A classic slab serif – one of the earliest – is Rockwell. It is well known as being a solid choice not only for headlines and signage, but also for logos.

CHOOSING FONTS

Fonts achieve two main things. Firstly, they visually interpret the voice of a piece of text. Secondly, they perform the technical job of recording text. These two functions cover both artistry and science – the nuanced job of conveying tone and the mechanical job of ensuring readability at the same time. Choosing the right typeface, and then using it carefully, will strike the important balance of art and science.

VISUAL VOICE

It goes without saying that an empty page in need of a typeface is a daunting thing. These days, there are so many – too many – options. New designs seem to be introduced daily. How does one avoid the endless scrolling? Identify your needs early.

3 MAY. BISTRITZ. Le1 arriving at Vienna ear at 6:46, but train was ; wonderful place, from the train and the little feared to go very far fi and would start as ne; impression I had was entering the East; the

THERE WAS NO POS: had been wanderir an hour in the mornin when there was no cor wind had brought wit! penetrating, that furth the question.

I was glad of it: I ne chilly afternoons: dre;

Above: Comparisons of the different types of typeface used in *Dracula* (left) and *Jane Eyre* (right).

Beyond the basics of legibility, choosing a font that embodies the character of the writing is what elevates basic typesetting to an art. On an intuitive level, the fonts you choose should give the reader a sense of the voice of the writing prior to reading a word. To use Victorian fiction as an example, at first glance, *Dracula* should look different from *Jane Eyre*. Or in corporate communications, the fonts used in marketing material for a children's hospital should contrast obviously with that of a mining company.

With Voice in Mind ...

The pointers below should help you choose the right font:

1. Determine the tone that is required. What impression must the design leave for readers? Let this tone help you in the process of elimination.

2. Use the font classification outlined in Chapter 2 as a way of narrowing your focus. Each classification has historical significance that embodies a style and way of thinking that can carry a piece of text into a deeper level of expression.

Below: An example of the Home Sweet Home Regular typeface, drawing creative attention to the advertised event.

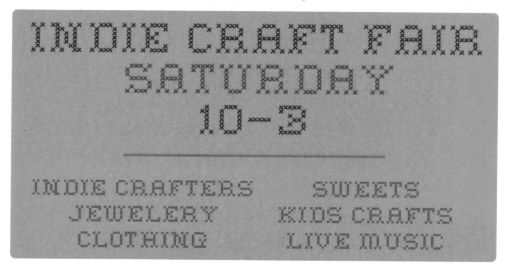

3. Be modest. It's easy to turn to overly stylized letterforms that express an idea literally. It is best to mix a highly decorative font with a modest, readable one – otherwise the font could draw attention to itself rather than the text.

TECHNICAL CONSIDERATIONS

Another important step in limiting your options is to state the more technical requirements of the text. Here are some questions to help clarify your non-creative needs.

In Print

If your project is to be printed, select a typeface that will read smoothly at the size it will be. Test your typeface by printing it out at full size. Everything looks great on a screen, but printing off your options and laying them beside each other gives you proper perspective. You need to see them in the same context in which they'll be read by the end user.

Web

Will it be read online? Typographic basics apply to both print and web, but web typography has added technological details that need addressing. Fonts for web design are thoroughly covered in Chapter 4, but it's worth noting here the process by which one selects fonts for screens.

Below: Verdana typeface clearly depicts letters with simple letterforms that are easy for onscreen reading.

1. Look for highly legible sans serif typefaces. Simple letterforms with large counters and tall x-heights read better at small sizes, and are excellent for onscreen reading. Many of the fonts included in your email settings have been designed to be read clearly onscreen.

2. Keep mindful of file size. Typefaces with large families or which can accommodate different languages, as handy as those are, have big file sizes, slowing a page's rendering time.

3. Check out the library of web fonts. Web fonts are downloaded by a browser while your web page is rendering – they are not fonts installed on to your own computer. This avenue ensures that your design will be readable and that the typeface you choose will be available.

4. If you don't use web fonts, test across browsers. Test across platforms. You have put a lot of thought into your design, and for a handful of users to experience it in any way other than what was intended would compromise your project and devalue your hard work.

Below: Adobe Caslon is a perfect typeface that can be highly legible at all sizes, weights and styles.

Adobe Caslon Pro
timeless and reliable
early EIGHTEENTH century
American Declaration of Independence
British Arts and Crafts movement
George Bernard Shaw

Adobe Caslon Pro Regular/Italic/Semibold/Semibold Italic/Bold/Bold Italic

Long Body Text

Pick a text font for projects comprising paragraphs, such as newspapers, books, journals, articles and so on. A good text typeface, such as Adobe Caslon, should have plenty of weights and styles (bolds, small caps, italics and so on), and be highly legible at smaller sizes. This topic is covered in full in Chapter 7.

Shorter Text

For captions, footnotes, bylines and so on – anything that is typically read at small sizes and in small doses – a clean, simple sans serif with a tall x-height and large counters should be considered. Another option is the italic style of your main text font.

Hierarchy

Typographic hierarchy performs the double duty of establishing a structure for reading, while providing visual interest and colour to your page. Perhaps your text includes headlines, captions, footnotes and subtitles, all of which have different levels of importance. Assigning both a style and size (see the illustration below) to each level organizes the information for the reader by way of contrast. Each level will need to have its own role and a style applied to that role consistently through the design. Once you know how many levels of information you have, you can be sure to pick a typeface that includes all the styles you need (italic, bold, bold italic and so on).

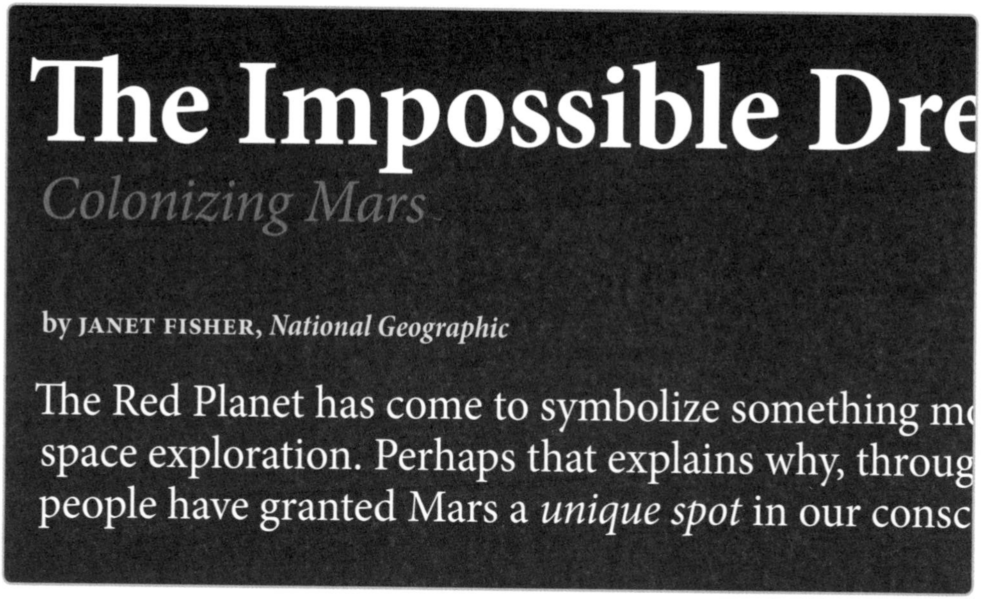

The Impossible Dre

Colonizing Mars

by **JANET FISHER**, *National Geographic*

The Red Planet has come to symbolize something m
space exploration. Perhaps that explains why, throug
people have granted Mars a *unique spot* in our consc

Above: A great representation of typographic hierarchy using a series of bold, italic, bold italic and regular Minion Pro typeface.

Size

Size applies to two things when it comes to fonts. Firstly, there is the size at which the text will be read – the font's point size. Secondly, there is the experimentation with size, which will impact its role in establishing hierarchy and texture/colours.

1. At what size will your font be read? How much text must you fit on your page or artboard? Define these and any questions related to size. A postage stamp, for example, requires a font with large counters and with little, if any, flourish. Choosing a font for a billboard needs bold, strong, large fonts, with thick lines that are highly readable at distances.

Canada
Christmas/Noël · 1996
60¢

Above: Univers Roman typeface is perfect for a postage stamp that requires a font with large counters.

Take note of how the shape of letters affects how large or small the font appears, regardless of its point size. Depending on the size of its x-height, and the lengths of its ascenders and descenders, a word in one font set in 12-point could look much bigger than a word in another font, also set in 12-point. Typefaces with a short x-height and tall ascenders and descenders will appear smaller than a typeface with a tall x-height and short ascenders and descenders. This is a great example of the balancing of technical traits required in typeface selection with the nuances and artistry of their designs.

Aa Bb Cc Dd Ee Ff Gg Hh Ii Jj Kk

Aa Bb Cc Dd Ee Ff Gg Hh Ii Jj Kk

Above: Really No. 2 Regular typeface (left) is represented at 72-point, and Perpetua Regular (right) is also represented at 72-point; both are the same size but look noticeably different due to the shape of the letters.

2. Variations in size give a design visual interest by way of contrast. Size also helps a reader understand what is most important, and helps them navigate a page (see 'Hierarchy', above). Playing is a simple way to discover unexpected results, so give yourself the freedom to experiment.

Characters

Are you working with another language or unusual symbols? Make sure you choose a typeface that includes all the characters your text requires. Each typeface has a chart of glyphs or characters, which maps out every single character included in the typeface – something you cannot access with the limited keys on your keyboard. If you are designing, you will need characters that include the accents used frequently in, for example, French.

FONT STYLES

After you've settled on some options, it is time to use the fonts. Various weights and styles that give structure and colour to your page are essential for the text to be as readable and interesting as possible.

Weight

Thin, light, medium, semibold, bold, extra bold ... On both sides of a typeface's regular weight are variations that come in handy when needing to emphasize a word or short phrase. These

Below: The Minion Pro Bold typeface, used here at the top, is more commonly used for titling and emphasizing a phrase than the Minion Pro Regular typeface, used here at the bottom, that is used more commonly for regular, extended information and text.

WORLD-LEADING TO WIN US TRIALS 200M FINAL

Justin Gatlin became the fifth-fastest 200m runne he won Sunday's final at the American Athletics.

THE 33-YEAR-OLD AMERICAN, who has served two doping bans, recorde seconds in Oregon. It bettered the 19.68 secs he ran in May which, at that in the world. Gatlin has been the dominant sprinter in 2015, having

weights should be chosen optically, because the difference between a regular weight and a bold might be more extreme than another. An extra bold, black or heavy font is typically best avoided for body text. These weights are suited for titling or large sizes.

Italics

Much like weight, an italic font is valuable for emphasis. But it also has grammatical significance, and when choosing a typeface that requires an italic, assess the italic on its own merit. Ask yourself firstly whether it is legible. Next, ask yourself whether it is attractive. Italic fonts that belong to quality typeface families are not simply slanted versions of the regular. They are designed especially to perform their task.

Right: A noticeable comparison of Didot Regular typeface represented in real small caps (left) and represented in false small caps (right).

ALL CAPS

| REAL SMALL CAPS | FALSE SMALL CAPS |

Small Caps

Like italics, well-crafted typefaces have had small capitals designed with great care, and not simply shrunken uppercase letters. Some design software includes a button that automatically changes text into false small caps. These lack the proportion of weight and size present in the real small caps. If there are abbreviations, acronyms, subtitles or short headings in your text, consider using small caps, but first be sure your chosen typeface includes them in its glyph map.

Below: Unlike the Bembo Book Regular typeface, represented to the right, the Trade Gothic Next Condensed typeface, represented to the left, allows a smoother read in small, narrow columns.

ECHOES Double star Circinus X-1 has produced the brightest x-ray light echoes (black rings) ever observed. Located 30,700 light-years from Earth, the system is nicknamed 'Lord of the Rings.'

ECHOES Double star Circinus X-1 has produced the brightest x-ray light echoes (black rings) ever observed. Located 30,700 light-years from Earth, the system is nicknamed 'Lord of the Rings.'

Condensed

Narrow columns are best read with condensed fonts, such as Trade Gothic or Myriad Pro Condensed. The narrow letterforms economically permit more words per line, and keep your eye from jumping down lines too frequently, making a smoother read.

Figures

If your project includes numerals, it's important to know what kind you will need. Lining numerals are designed for charts, maths and equations. Old Style numerals are designed to be read in body text, and have qualities similar to that of letters. Again, check the glyph map to make sure what you need is available.

123
45
678
90

123
45
678
90

Above: This shows Centaur Pro Regular lining figures typeface (left), generally designed for charts, and the Centaur Pro Regular Old Style figures typeface (right), generally designed to match the letters in a body of text.

Ligatures

In order to look balanced, some letters overlap when set next to each other. For example, the ascender of the lowercase 'f' hits the dot of the lowercase 'i' (as in the example shown here). This problem was solved hundreds of years ago with the designing of ligatures, the pairing of certain letters into a single character. These are often but not always automatically applied in the typesetting of body text. Check the font before you buy.

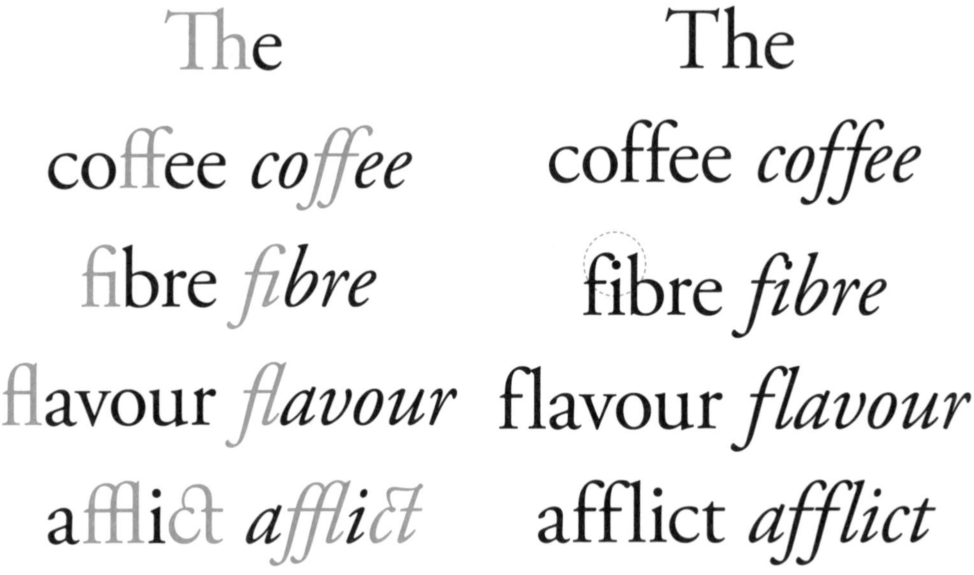

The

coffee *coffee*

fibre *fibre*

flavour *flavour*

afflict *afflict*

The

coffee *coffee*

fibre *fibre*

flavour *flavour*

afflict *afflict*

Above: Shown here is a clear representation of the Centaur Pro Regular and Italic typeface with ligatures (left) that overlap other letters in the text, and without ligatures (right) that automatically separate letters from one another.

Colour

Printing technologies are advanced and generally reliable, but fonts with thin strokes may not read as well printed reversed (such as white on black). Traditionally, ink would overwhelm the letterform if the typeface was too thin. Print tests to make sure your design works.

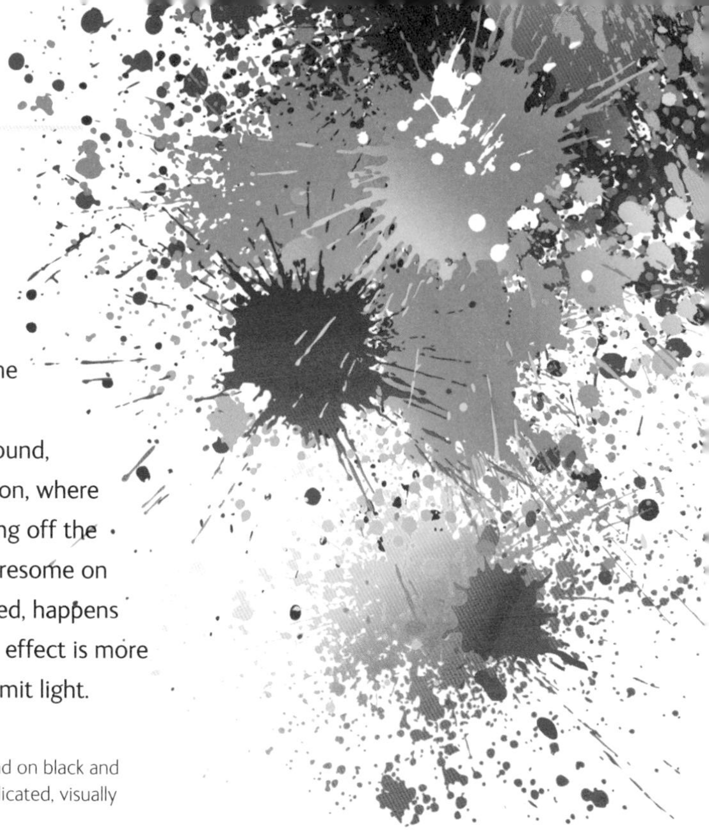

Readability of text is greatly affected by the colours you choose to apply. Like size, experimenting with colour yields exciting results but there are some colour combinations you can rule out. Blue and/or green text on a red background, and vice versa, results in a visual vibration, where the letters look as though they are sitting off the background. It is difficult to read and tiresome on our eyes. Chromostereopsis, as it is called, happens in both printed and online text, but the effect is more pronounced on screens because they emit light.

Below: Minion Pro Regular text is far easier to read on black and white printed colours (left) than it is on the complicated, visually vibrating green and red printed colours (right).

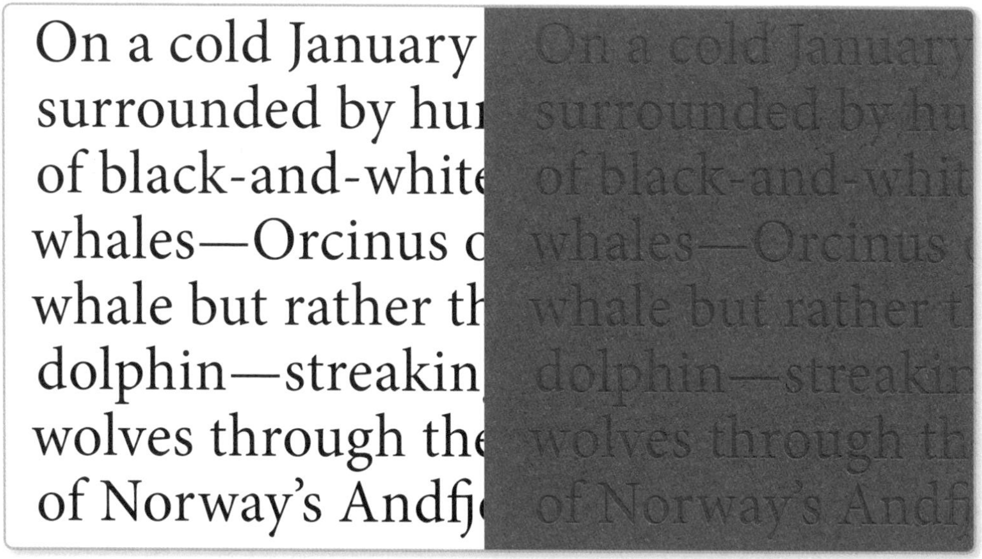

On a cold January
surrounded by hu
of black-and-white
whales—Orcinus o
whale but rather th
dolphin—streakin
wolves through the
of Norway's Andfj

Be Mindful of Typesetting

It expands the topic of this book, but typesetting influences the choosing of fonts. This includes leading (the spaces between lines of text) and kerning (the space between individual letters). Some typefaces require more work to arrange. Here's an example: if you're designing a gig poster that needs to be bold and dense, a typeface with distinctly tall ascenders and descenders demands generous leading (the space in between the lines of text) or they will collide. But choosing a strong typeface and setting it in all caps ensures a strong block of text that is both readable and legible.

Quick Tip

Find excellent examples of designs that have successfully used legible typefaces. And remember that there is a difference between display typefaces and ornamental typefaces.

Above: Shown clearly here, the Futura Condensed Medium in title case (left) has unequal leading and kerning, whereas the Futura Condensed Medium in all caps (right) has strong text that is both readable and legible.

FONT COMBINATIONS

In combining fonts, you want to achieve a liveliness that reflects the content. The key is finding fonts that complement each other, not compete.

TIPS

Before we outline what makes a successful combination of fonts, here are a few tips.

Symmetry

Some designers test out font pairings by typing out a nonsense word in order to assess how the shapes and arrangements work together, without being distracted by reading the word. One common trick is typing a word in one font, and then using the second font to type the word backwards to compare the typefaces' symmetry.

Gabocse escobaG

Above: A common designer test is represented here: typing a word in Century Regular typeface (left) and typing the same word backwards in another typeface, Futura Medium (right) to assess and compare how shapes and arrangements work together.

Shape

Another tool is the transposing of fonts on top of each other, applying a transparency or screen, and noting how their respective geometries complement each other. From this, terminal endings, axis tilt and line weights are all evident.

Gabocse

Above: The transparency of the Adobe Garamond in pink clearly complements the Chaparral Pro in blue.

Exercise Restraint

Be wary of using too many fonts. Unless the design objective includes the purposeful use of many different typefaces, it is often good to limit your font usage to two or three, while using the weight and style differences included in each typeface to provide added interest. This can be difficult, given today's endless supply of typeface options so readily available, but in doing so, your project will be noticeably more refined and professional.

Time and Testing

Give yourself type-testing time. As mentioned above, print off the combinations at full size and let your intuition speak to you. It is possible to arrive at a solution quickly, but do not expect it.

PICKING PAIRS

The following six points will help you focus and make the task of font-hunting a pleasant and rewarding part of your design process.

Use One Font – a Superfont

One of the most obvious (and safe) font pairing strategies is to use the many different weights and styles of one large type family. These families are aptly known as superfamilies. Choosing a single typeface that includes a vast number of weights, styles and character options (glyphs) can satisfy all hierarchical needs.

There are some superfonts that include serif and sans serif variations. These large families have the potential to provide the contrast and colour you're looking for, while establishing a strong visual consistency.

Above: The superfonts here have many serif and sans serif variations that create the Frutiger Sans and Frutiger Serif into a superfamily.

This method is safe. Experimenting with size and colour is very important to ensure your design is effective and that your hierarchy is not lost in similar fonts. Push for contrast with this method to achieve a dynamic design.

Similar in Shape

Choosing two fonts that share a similar construction, such as Garamond and Chapparal, can provide uniform flow of tone. Notice how they both have a similar cap height, x-height and the same length of ascenders/descenders. Note their similar angles and how their strokes are in proportion to each other. See how they share a similar width. Yet their differences are substantial enough to provide visual interest and colour.

Mary Lamb

the EMINENT WOMEN SERIES

by MRS. GILCHRIST   *Ed.* JOHN H. INGRAM

Preface

I am indebted to Mrs. Henry Watson, a granddaughter of Mr. Gillman, for one or two interesting reminiscences, and for a hitherto unpublished "notelet" by Lamb (p. 248), together with an omitted paragraph from a published letter (p. 84), which confirms what other letters also show,--that the

Above: A combination of the similarly constructed Garamond and Chapparal typfaces through a series of bold, italic, condensed italic, and regular fonts in order to provide a visually appealing page.

Avoid Sharing Distinctions

Be sure to avoid choosing two fonts with the same features that make the fonts distinct. An example would be the use of two slab serif typefaces. Slabs typically have visually strong features. Vista Slab and Clarendon speak over each other – they are too similar and therefore too loud when used together.

Contrast

Two fonts with dramatic differences can infuse your design with an energy that conveys your confidence as a designer. Some reliable combinations include choosing a distinctly interesting typeface and a neutral one. Refer back to the font classification section in Chapter 2, and purposefully avoid pairing fonts belonging to the same classification.

BANISH CLUTTER
How to Organize Every Room in Your Home   by Tom Bonnett

Our organizational home tour starts in the living room, which is wh ing, hanging out, and happiest memory-making takes place. Here, y tive, clear-eyed view of your clutter and how it impacts your every solidating all of your electronics in one custom cabinet and use lin the television when it's not in use.

Above: Try not to use fonts that have too much in common, as here with Clarendon and Vista Slab, otherwise the result is in danger of being too visually 'shouty'.

Dame Kiri Te Kanawa opera masterclass

26 JUNE 2015

As part of the BBC Cardiff Singer of the World season, i opera star Dame Kiri Te Kanawa leads a masterclass for

DAME KIRI WORKS WITH SINGERS, Celine Forrest, Blaise Malaba, Regu grim and offers a critique on both voice and performance in the Dora Stou College of Music and Drama. Accompaniment is provided by pianist Simo

Above: Combining two dramatically different fonts, such as Universe Pro Bold and Italic and Bembo, will energize a design.

Typeface Designer

Like all artists and craftspeople, typeface designers have their own distinct styles. They dedicate their careers to developing new typefaces, but their collection of work will most likely channel their personality or philosophy of design, resulting in forms that naturally suit each other. Eric Gill is the genius behind Gill Sans, Perpetua and Joanna. Try Adrian Frutiger's Univers and Egyptienne, or Hermann Zapf's Optima and Palatino. Minion and Myriad make excellent companions, and are the designs of Robert Slimbach. This requires a little research but is well worth the effort.

HOURS & RATES

Regular Hours		MOV Admission Rates	
		All prices include applicable sales tax.	
Monday	10 AM-5 PM	Adult	£24
Tuesday	10 AM-5 PM	Student	£15
Wednesday	10 AM-5 PM	Senior	£15 (age 65+)
Thursday	10 AM-8 PM	Youth	£10 (ages 5-18)
Friday	10 AM-5 PM		
Saturday	11 AM-5 PM		
Sunday	11 AM-5 PM		

Above: Represented is an excellent example of a good typeface combination: Myriad Pro Bold and Minion.

Historical Pairing

Fonts designed in the same historical era often share a theoretical and technical foundation. Under what technical circumstances were the typefaces designed? Are they letterforms based on calligraphic standards or were they designed for the not-so-long-ago days of photosetting?

Some typefaces have been designed as revivals of a much older style. Transitional serif typefaces, such as Perpetua, from the mid-1700s, have strong vertical strokes and axis, and were intentional departures from the calligraphic tradition. It was the Enlightenment, after all. This more graphic, calculated

COLD DISHES

Lightly cured Spring salmon
Rye, dill, smoked roe creme fraiche

16

Torchon of duck foie gras
Strawberry, elderflower, sour brioche

24

WARM DISHES

Snails and crispy chicken skin
Charleston gold rice, parsley, garlic

17

Roast scallops and mushrooms
Warm custard and cress

18

Pan fried veal sweetbreads on toast
Sauce gribiche with veal tongue

15

Baked Pacific oysters
Whipped garlic butter, truffle

18

Above: A good historical pairing is represented here through the use of Perpetua and Avenir typefaces.

approach lends itself well to geometric sans serif typefaces from the 1920s – or modern rivals such as Avenir – which were themselves rejecting the ornamentation of the past.

Do your homework and consult the font classification guide in Chapter 2 to identify which fonts belong to which era. Also, note that the more specifically a typeface references a historical period, the more important it is to reserve that typeface for era-specific writing.

Intuition

Trust yourself. If it feels right, it probably is. If something seems off, mix things up and try the unexpected. Being surprised by something unconventional is how exciting design happens. Allow yourself to make mistakes and have fun. With practice, you will intuitively begin to recognize how and why some fonts work together, and why others do not. Pay attention to how your eyes respond to the text you have just arranged. Are they at peace? Good.

Quick Tip

In the end, does it feel right? Does it function well? If you can say 'yes' to both, you have something to work with.

A GOOD STARTING POINT

There are so many typefaces available these days that it seems as though the main task in choosing fonts is narrowing down one's options. Focusing early in the design process is the best way to turn what seems at first to be an overwhelming task into an enjoyable, fun and creative exercise.

CONTEXT

It goes without saying that your typographic decisions must be justified on the basis of the material. It has been stressed repeatedly, but it is such an important point – it cannot be stressed enough. Apart from the tonal, technical and traditional ways to select fonts, there are other areas grounded on the content that can enrich your design. Not only does this extra digging pay respect to the text, but it also unveils subtle design characteristics that, together with the text, can achieve a unified project – integrated design. Building upon the points covered thus far, here are some places to jump from.

Above: The 1960 text, Eurostile Regular and Bold, makes the poster appear as if it originated from that time period.

Date the Text

Is there a strong historical aspect to the text you're working with? Perhaps it was written in the 1960s. Or maybe it was written four months ago but is an article about car design in the 1960s. A quick scan through typefaces published during that time yields a classic: Eurostile. As a title font, it could suit both the topic and the time very well. Take some time and read up on what design features originated in the time referenced in the writing, and discern their appropriateness for the text. A match could be made.

Place the Text

Similar to above, a location represented in a piece of writing can help focus your options. Geography plays a major role in the story of type design, and there are plenty of regional qualities that can be highlighted to enhance the writing. Perhaps you are tasked with designing the cover for a book about the wines of northern Italy. Bodoni is a font originating in the region, and would suit the topic and speak the same cultural visual language.

Above: Bodoni, a typeface that originated in Italy, is a logical choice here for a piece on Italian culture.

Theme

Some general themes, not exclusive to time or place, have developed their own visual cues. You are designing the invitation for a wedding with a nautical theme. The fundraiser will feature jazz musicians. The heritage centre's grand opening has a Western theme. Do be careful not to rely on highly ornamental interpretations of a theme. There is a difference between choosing a font, the letters of which are composed from lassos, and a typeface based on the woodcut designs of nineteenth-century America.

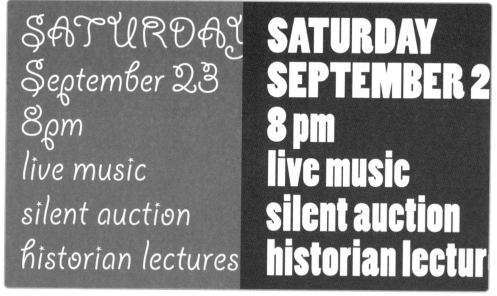

Above: The Giddyup typeface (left) and the Poplar typeface (right) can both be developed into a specific theme for certain designs.

The Underlying Subject

Like all artistic disciplines, typography has always embodied the spirit of an epoch. It might require more research on your part, but for text with a philosophical or political message, selecting fonts that reflect the same thinking is worth considering. Perhaps you are choosing a typeface for an article about Germany, leading up to the Second World War.

Examining the potential of some of Paul Renner's work might lead to a suitable typeface. As a vocal opponent of Nazism, his designs also aesthetically opposed the growing movement by purposefully avoiding historical letterforms that were believed to represent an ideal Germany. Consequently, after the release of his famous Futura, and one particularly scathing publication, he was deemed a traitor.

BAD STARTING POINTS

Within all these suggested starting points is still the risk of slipping into the rut of choosing a font that all too literally reflects a theme. This is most obvious in ornamental display fonts that are designed to be seen first and read second. Here are two cautionary tips to be mindful of in your exploration of themes.

Easy Street

Quality aside, the name of a font does not indicate what sort of text it should be given. Lithos, based on the letterforms of ancient Greece, is found on most computers. To select it for anything related to Greece (a Greek cookbook, travel guide or textbook, for instance) is a weak choice, not only because of its obvious relationship to the subject, but also because of its ubiquity. Applying only a little more effort would open up both the subject and the design possibilities, and yield a more thoughtful and therefore stronger design.

MIXED NUT & HONEY BAKLAVA

SWEET FILO PASTRY TREATS

1. PREHEAT THE OVEN TO 180C. PLACE ALL T
SYRUP INGREDIENTS IN A MEDIUM SAUCEP/
WITH 300ML OF WATER AND BRING TO A
TLE SIMMER. LET IT BUBBLE AWAY, STIRRIN(
SIONALLY, FOR 15 MINUTES OR UNTIL THE

Above: Using the ubiquitous Lithos Pro for a Greek-related subject can be a weak choice – try to be a little more original.

Not Punny

Typographic puns are also something to be wary of. They are either inside jokes between designers, or quick and lazy solutions to a typeface dilemma. An example of this is seen in the 2012 film *Lawless*, set in 1931 in Franklin, Virginia. The captions were set in Franklin Gothic. This is not a particularly terrible choice – historical parallels could be found – but was it a nod to the in-house production team?

DESIGN & COPYRIGHT OF FONTS

What makes typeface design so fascinating is how much variation is possible, while still making the symbols on which we base our communication interesting, interpretive and functional.

TYPEFACE DESIGN

Designing typefaces is a careful and important job. With the explosion in software democratizing the design of letterforms, it is more important than ever to narrow your searches to reliable foundries that have excellent designers on staff or have contracts with reputable typeface designers.

Above: Do buy fonts through font foundries to ensure that you don't fall foul of the law.

As it will be stressed below, it is very important that all fonts are purchased legitimately through foundries, the companies that design, produce and distribute fonts, or through reputable third-party suppliers.

COPYRIGHT

Intellectual property and copyright laws are complicated and, frankly, a tedious read. But like all forms of art, typeface designers create original work, which deserves protection and remuneration. Whoever owns the copyright can reproduce their work as they wish. They can also license their right for a fee. That is how we use and benefit from the work of typeface designers.

Intellectual Property

Copyright law differs from country to country. Reading the End User Licence Agreement before your purchase is essential. Germany and England, for example, protect the artistic design of a complete typeface (all the characters). In the United States, only the font software is protected, not the typeface as a design.

Font Licences

Some font licences allow for installation on up to five computers. Other licences limit it to one. Before purchasing, know how many people will need access to the font files and budget accordingly. Depending on how much you can spend, licensing may be a factor when deciding which fonts to use.

Above: Each foundry will have its own rules as to how many computers can use a particular font, so always check the fine print before you buy.

Font Piracy

Software piracy is generally understood to be a no-no. But did you know that your font files are software? What can you not do?

1. Share font files.
2. Copy font files.
3. Include copies of the fonts in your working files.

The last point needs added explanation. When preparing your design files for printing, your layout program packages all the design elements that you have used in your design (photographs, illustrations and fonts). With all these pieces, your printer can prepare your project. It is illegal for a printer to use your packaged fonts without a licence of its own. Thankfully, today it is common for printers to accept files with design elements embedded in a PDF. Embedding fonts ensures font files are used legally and your typesetting stays perfectly set after it leaves your desk.

Aperçu — Light	Aperçu — Light Italic	Aperçu — Regular
Aperçu — Regular Italic	Aperçu — Medium	Aperçu — Medium Italic
Aperçu — Bold	Aperçu — Bold Italic	Aperçu — Mono
Archive — Roman	Archive — Roman Italic	Archive — Semibold
Archive — Semibold Italic	Archive — Bold	Archive — Bold Italic
Archive — Extra Bold	Archive — Extra Bold Italic	Archive — Mono
Basis Grot — Light NEW!	Basis Grot — Light Italic NEW!	Basis Grot — Off White NEW!

Above: With so many fonts readily available online, it is easy to download a font illegally by mistake, so do ensure you are not committing piracy.

Be a thoughtful designer by honouring the work of typeface designers and foundries. Buy all your fonts and adhere to the contract you signed at the time of purchase. Do not share your fonts and do not accept fonts if offered by others.

FONT PURCHASING

You have selected your fonts. You are ready to commit. There are some rather dull details included in the selection of a font, and unless you have a particular interest in software, the details might be boring. But it is important to know just enough in order to buy the right file for your computer.

Buying Fonts for Desktop

Fonts are little computer programs. Thanks to technology and corporate competition, there are a few formats that you will run across before getting to the till.

AaBbQq
fly fishing
Beatification
26 Anesthesiologists
relevant to propioception
Rodomontade is my favorite. Means boastful.

1. Type1, a format by Adobe, is also known as PostScript. They are sometimes called outline fonts – fonts based on lines and curves, making their rendering at different sizes accurate and fast. When you purchase a Type1 font, you must specify whether it will be used on a PC or a Mac – they are not cross-platform fonts.

Left: PostScript fonts are outline vector fonts, and can be scaled to virtually any size.

ABCD
KLMN
ABCD
HIJK

2. TrueType fonts (TTF) were developed by Microsoft and Apple in the 1980s. Also outline fonts, this formatting allowed a font to be viewed at different sizes by adjusting its pixels in relation to its outline, and they are generally associated with being ideal for online viewing. The TrueType file extension is .ttf, and these fonts are not cross-platform either. Check twice before you buy.

Left: OpenType fonts are an extension of the TrueType format, with advanced typography features.

3. OpenType (the file extension is .oft) is a wrapper, in that it contains the technology of both Type1 and TTF but works on both PC and Mac platforms. It also has superior capability to meet very detailed typographic and linguistic challenges.

Right: Typekit is an example of one of the many typeface subscription services available.

Buying Fonts for the Web

There are two main ways for website designers to choose and use typefaces. Both services are reliable in that their products are all optimized for web use, have fonts supplied by reputable foundries, and have been instrumental in bringing typographic sophistication to the web. See the next chapter for more on web fonts.

1. Subscription-based typeface use is becoming very popular, with a service called Typekit, which embeds fonts into your designs. A subscriber pays for a single licensing agreement. It is included in Adobe's Creative Cloud products.

2. You can also buy single web fonts without a subscription. There are services (Fontspring, for example) that supply the fonts for all your websites and include perpetual licensing.

Below: Fontspring will supply a wide variety of entitled fonts for websites.

FONT FOUNDRIES

Like anything, you develop a taste for quality the more you are exposed to it. If you start your typeface collection by relying on established and reliable foundries, and keep yourself familiar with the timeless classics, you will grow to recognize a quality typeface.

WHAT IS A FOUNDRY?

Companies that design, produce and sell typefaces are called foundries. Traditionally, foundries manufactured the metal and wood typefaces that were printed on wood and iron printing presses. The contemporary foundry does the same thing but now with digital files. Just because a typeface has been designed and has a copyright does not mean that every font is worthy. It is important to source your fonts from quality type foundries.

First-rate Foundries

Almost as old as the history of printing is the history of foundries. Some of the most established companies to date have been instrumental in moving the world of typography through several technological epochs, not the least of which is the digital age. They have seen a great deal of change and provide the design world with a wealth of understanding. Here is a list of some of the most reputable foundries:

- Linotype
- Monotype
- Apple
- Adobe
- ITC (International Typeface Corporation

New Faces

Building on the legacy of others, there are new foundries that have challenged and enhanced type design. Here are some of the quality newer foundries:

- Émigré
- Hoefler and Co.
- Frere-Jones Type
- Type Together
- House Industries

- Typotheque
- Font Bureau
- The Dutch Type Library
- Commercial Type
- Underware

Budget Conscious

Some fonts are less expensive than others. How have these foundries been able to sell at a lesser cost? Some, such as Bitstream (part of Monotype), have created adaptations of classic fonts normally available via more established foundries, like the ones listed above. Others, such as Lost Type, have developed a co-op – a pay-what-you-want model, with all the proceeds going directly to the designers.

Free Fonts

Remember – you get what you pay for. Free fonts have been, until recently, poorly designed and lacking the basic weights and styles that we now know are essential for planning and executing a design project. It's no surprise that the influx of free fonts coincided with the sudden accessibility of font design software to designers with no formal training in typeface design. People were making fonts for fun and making them available for free. While the origin of this is not in any way sinister, it did result in a decline in the quality of graphic design. Just because one can use something, it doesn't mean one should.

Google Fonts

But things have changed yet again with Google Fonts (*see* the section on web fonts on page 118). Google commissions fonts for open-source projects and releases them licence- and cost-free. Open-source advocates are fully supportive, and on

occasion a professional typeface designer shares their work. The typefaces are generally well designed and include the standard numbers of weights, styles and characters.

Quick Tip

Google WebFonts are ideal for web-based design. Print designers, though, should stick with the foundries above.

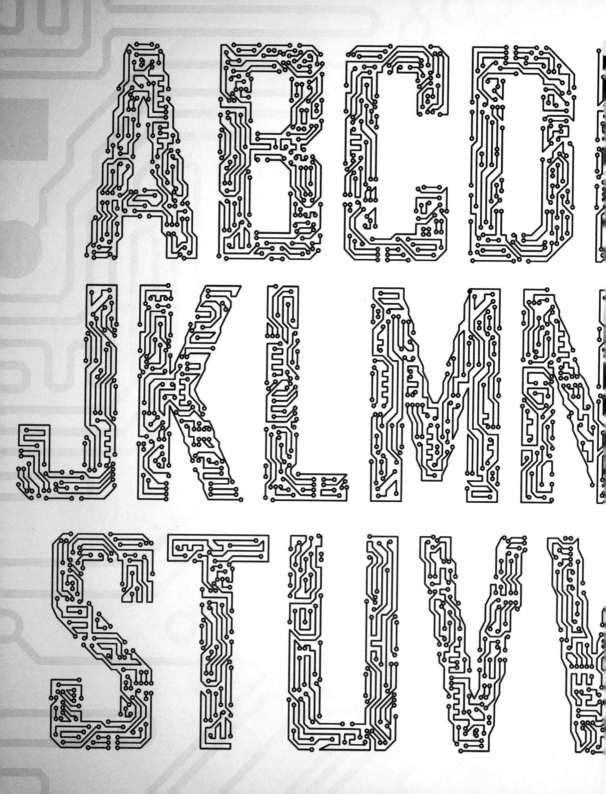

WEB & MOBILE FONTS

WEB VS PRINT FONTS

It hasn't been very long since choosing fonts for use on the web meant a very slim selection of web-safe fonts that were common to all operating systems and browsers.

This meant that typographers and designers were limited to the lowest common denominator of around five or six fonts, including Arial, Verdana, Times, Georgia and Courier.

Above: Choosing a font to use on a web page has become as easy as finding one for use in print.

THINGS ARE MUCH BETTER NOW!

Thankfully, things have moved on dramatically in the past few years, and today it's common to see as diverse a range of fonts on a web page as you might find in print. A range of free and subscription services have sprung up, and web browsers have adopted standards that make choosing fonts for the web for the right aesthetic reasons far easier.

WHERE DO YOU START?

Just as in print, there is are a host of considerations to keep in mind when choosing which font or combination of fonts you might use in a project. This ranges from the device your work will be viewed on to issues of licensing, legibility and, of course, the all-important aesthetic considerations too. Web typography doesn't offer quite the same level of fine control as print, but sometimes limitations lead to innovation.

DEVICE-DRIVEN DESIGN

Designing typography for the screen is an entirely different discipline from designing for print. This is because the screen offers the opportunity to change the content's presentation, while the appearance of print is predetermined at the point it goes to press.

Typically, when designing a website, for example, we tend to think of one particular type of device that will be used to access and view the pages. The truth is that any number of different devices could be used to access a site, which brings a number of unique challenges to the design process.

TAILORING DISPLAY TO THE MEDIUM

Nowadays, you're as likely to be accessing a website via a smartphone as a laptop, or a games console rather than a desktop computer. Each different device has its own unique properties in terms of resolution, system fonts, memory and support for web standards.

Best Practice: Control your Measure

The width of a text column can strongly impact on its readability. In print, columns are typically set to contain anything between 50 and 75 characters (which is approximately 9 to 15 words wide). This is considered to be the ideal

Above: Web-connected devices come in many different sizes and forms.

Quick Tip

An em is broadly representative of the space an uppercase letter M occupies in a particular font, at a particular size. In practice, an em represents the font size itself – so using type set at 12-point, one em would be 12-point regardless of font choice. Ems are proportional to the font size, so as the font size increases or decreases, the size of an em follows suit, making it a useful relative measure.

width for text, enabling the reader to easily move between lines without losing their place. The same general rules apply on the web, so aim to set your type in columns of no more than around 80 characters wide. Remember that you can set your column width in ems; use the CSS code: `width:80em;`

CONSIDERATIONS WHEN DESIGNING FOR DEVICES

There are a host of things you need to keep in mind and cater for when designing for different devices and screen sizes. These considerations range from the resolution of the device, to the orientation, and whether a particular device applies anti-aliasing (smoothing) to fonts.

Stick to the Golden Rules

In general, all the basic best-practice advice and rules that apply to typography design for print also apply in the digital sphere. The same principles of providing space between lines of type, restricting the length of each line, choosing a font that aids legibility, and considering readability all apply.

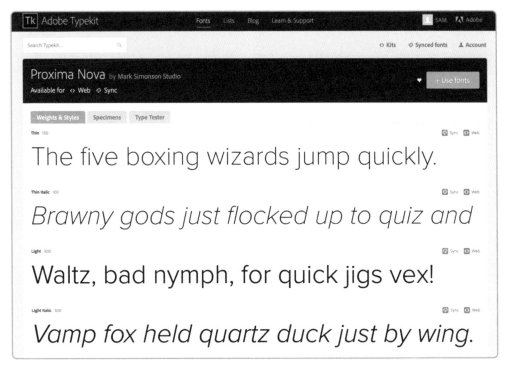

Above: Some fonts work more successfully on smaller screens than others, so choose to suit the device you're targeting.

Sans Serifs Work Best

In addition to these basic rules, however, you need to bear in mind that a screen pushes light out (with the exception of E Ink screens, such as those found on the Kindle), and this impacts on a screen's ability to display serifs legibly. As a result, the general consensus is that sans serif fonts with a large x-height are easier to read onscreen than more traditional serif fonts.

You Can't Control Everything

Don't forget that some users may override the settings you provide with your website, choosing to render your content in their own choice of font. This can be problematic if you're trying to convey meaning through your font. The same goes for colour schemes. Visually impaired users may well have a high-contrast colour palette that is applied to all content on their device to improve legibility.

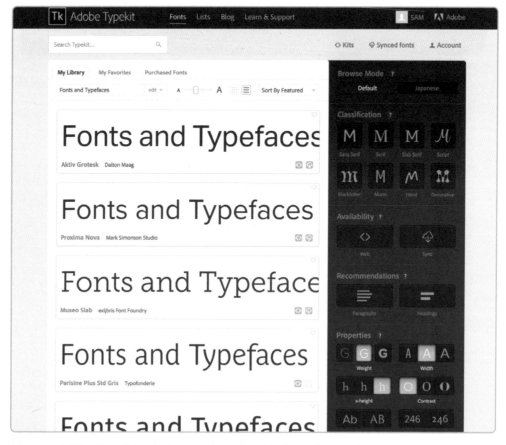

Above: Adobe's TypeKit service makes it easy to choose fonts based on attributes such as contrast.

WHAT MAKES A WEB FONT A WEB FONT?

Almost any font could be used on the web. What makes a web font a web font in particular is its ability to be easily distributed for use on a web page. There are other considerations, too:

1. Fonts designed for use on the web may make more extensive use of unicode and the extended character sets required for non-Latin languages.

2. Hinting may be optimized for screen display, so the font automatically kerns differently from a print-orientated font.

3. The font may not contain the full set of ligatures you might find in a print-orientated font, because these are more difficult to display and may not render properly on all devices.

4. The font may be packaged in such a way as to facilitate limited use, according to the terms of the licence being granted to the designer.

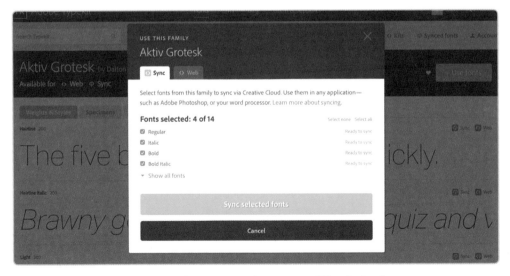

Above: Using a font on the web is as simple as copying and pasting some CSS and/or JavaScript into your page.

DIFFERENCES BETWEEN PLATFORMS

We know intuitively that a desktop computer offers a very different user experience compared to a smartphone or tablet, but this has a particular effect on how typography works for the reader. Check out the comparison table below for an explanation of the basic differences to consider.

Smartphone	Tablet	Laptop/Desktop	TV
Small physical screen, high resolution.	Small physical screen, high resolution.	Medium-sized physical screen, high resolution.	Very large physical screen, but typically lower resolution.
Fonts need to be bigger relatively to ensure they're large enough to read on a small screen.	Fonts can be rendered at a similar size to those on a laptop or desktop computer.	These screens were designed to be utilitarian, displaying type comfortably.	Not ideal for displaying text. Type looks soft, and with reduced legibility.
Often leading-edge browsers that support modern CSS standards, allowing for safe use of web fonts.	Often leading-edge browsers that support modern CSS standards, allowing for safe use of web fonts.	Many older computers continue to be used to browse the web, especially in the corporate environment. These may not support web fonts.	Typically feature bespoke web browsers that are designed to provide basic access rather than a full web experience. Limitations may apply.
Device-specific fonts may overrule any font choices you specify.	Device-specific fonts may overrule any font choices you specify.	Device-specific fonts may overrule any font choices you specify.	Device-specific fonts may overrule any font choices you specify.
Users have the ability to set their own choice of fonts and colour schemes.	Users have the ability to set their own choice of fonts and colour schemes.	Users have the ability to set their own choice of fonts and colour schemes.	Users have the ability to set their own choice of fonts and colour schemes.

THE BEST FONT FOR YOUR PROJECT

The same rules apply to choosing fonts for devices as for print. First, you need to consider your users and make sure that you are tailoring your aesthetic choices to match their needs and expectations. Once you've ticked that off, apply the basic golden rules of typography ...

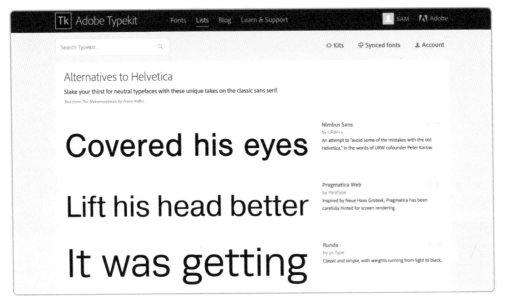

Above: Choosing a good font can be a matter of personal taste, but there are plenty of great alternatives to the old faithful favourites.

Less is More

Choose one base font, and one display font, and try to stick to those. Just because there are thousands of fonts available, it doesn't mean you have to use them all in your design.

Stick to Fonts Designed for Purpose

There's no point using a display font for your paragraph copy, because display fonts have been designed to be used at larger point sizes – ideal as headlines, but not optimized for reading large passages.

Choose Appropriate Fonts

Make sure you choose fonts that are appropriate for your subject matter – a script font might work well to represent a handwritten letter, but it's not going to give a professional impression if you're using it on a corporate website.

MAKE YOUR WEBSITE RESPOND TO DIFFERENT DEVICES

A big buzzword on the web in recent times has been the concept of responsive design. This idea allows for content to be repaginated to suit the individual device being used to view it. This might alter the layout, exclude some superfluous elements or dramatically change the typographical treatment.

Responsive Design

Responsive design is a simple concept, and it's pretty straightforward to implement using just CSS if you have a user demographic that uses modern web browsers. Check out the example below that shows how to use different font settings according to the width of the user's screen.

Left: Responsive design allows you to control how your content is seen on different devices.

1. Start by designing your website as you normally would, and create a set of base CSS styles to control your typography. Bear in mind that subsequent rules will cascade back to your basic set of instructions, so keep things as device-agnostic as possible. If you've got a typical device that's most commonly used to access your site, it's OK to engineer your basic styles to suit that specific device.

2. Add an @media clause to your stylesheet, as shown. This limits all the rules contained within the brackets to devices that fit the profile shown.

```
@media all and (max-width: 640px) {...}
```

The net result of the above code is that any rules you place within the section marked {...} are only used by devices that have a horizontal resolution of up to 640 pixels.

Donec ullamcorper nulla non metus auctor fringilla. Aenean eu leo quam. Pellentesque ornare sem lacinia quam venenatis vestibulum. Donec id elit non mi porta gravida at eget metus. Nullam id dolor id nibh ultricies vehicula ut id elit. Donec ullamcorper nulla non metus auctor fringilla. Nullam id dolor id nibh

Donec ullamcorper nulla non metus auctor fringilla. Aenean eu leo quam. Pellentesque ornare sem lacinia quam venenatis vestibulum. Donec id elit non mi porta gravida at eget metus. Nullam id dolor id nibh ultricies vehicula ut id elit. Donec ullamcorper nulla non metus auctor fringilla. Nullam id dolor id nibh ultricies vehic-

Above: Type can be changed to suit the device profile by using @media queries in your stylesheet.

3. Iterate and test. Start by setting an obvious attribute to check that you're targeting devices correctly. For example, set the colour of the text to be red on devices with a small screen. Once you've established that you are able to specify rules according to the device, develop your own typographical treatment to suit each different device profile you wish to target.

```
@media all and (max-width: 640px) {color:red;}
```

KEY CONSIDERATIONS

There are many nuances to typography, and almost every bit of advice in this book can be applied to the screen as well as the printed page. There are some device-specific considerations, however, that are worth reiterating. If you ensure you've considered each of these aspects for your choice of fonts, you won't go too far wrong.

Screen Orientation

The orientation of a screen has an impact on line length and readability. Smartphones in portrait orientation cannot display the same number of words per line of type as a desktop computer can. Make your design responsive to take these differences in screen real estate into account.

Below: Sans serif fonts are in theory easier to read on screens.

Legibility is Different Onscreen

Traditional thinking holds that serif fonts are easier to read than sans serif fonts, because the addition of the serifs helps provide a pointer to which letterform is being used. There's debate over how much of this is science and how much is simply cultural. On the web and screen, the debate swings the other way. In general, sans serif fonts are considered easier to read because a screen pushes out light that bleeds into serifs. Again, the truth is up for debate. Some fonts do indeed work better onscreen than in print, and vice versa, so consider carefully the legibility of your chosen fonts when designing for screen.

WEB FONTS MUST BE DOWNLOADED

Web fonts are just like any other asset you include on your website, and must be downloaded to the device being used to display it. This is fine if your users are all benefiting from fast Wi-Fi with no restrictions, but less so if they're relying on old-fashioned GPRS data connections. Remember that each time you use a different font, you're adding to the weight of the page, so the less-is-more maxim is worth bearing in mind for speed as well as aesthetic reasons.

Below: All web font services show you the download size, so you can ensure you're not making your pages too heavy.

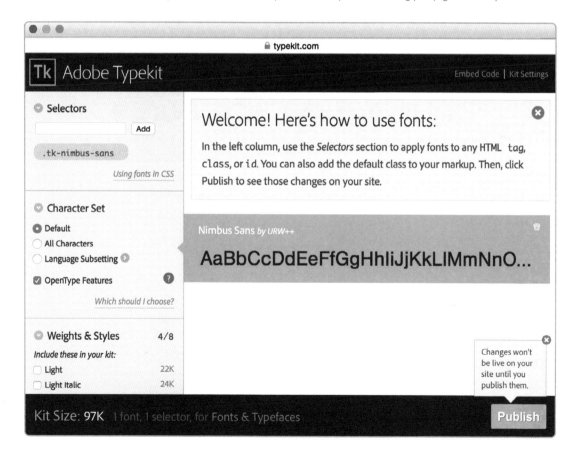

USING WEB FONTS

Over the past few years, the use of web fonts beyond the traditional set of five or six common web-safe options has exploded. In many ways, it's now easier for web designers to legitimately and cost-effectively use a wide range of fonts than their print-confined colleagues.

HOW THEY WORK

When you utilize a web font on your page, you're providing the font as a file that is downloaded by your browser as an asset, just like any other on the page. Depending upon the system being employed, the browser may only keep the file for that particular session, or it

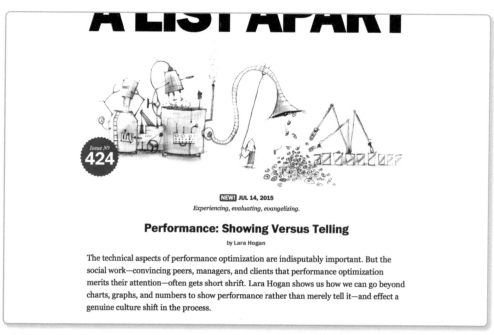

Above: The A List Apart website is a typographically led design that also features useful articles on type in the browser.

may cache the font file for later reuse. The most common method for loading a font is via CSS, although commercial font providers might use JavaScript to load the font into the page, because this allows the font licensor to check that the font is being used legitimately.

Regardless of the delivery mechanism, however, the principle remains the same. A file is downloaded and used to display the content using the chosen font. As a result, there is a risk that if you choose too many fonts, or fonts that have too large a file size, there will be a flash associated with the browser-rendering content using the default browser font, before the chosen web font has finished downloading. Most premium web font services provide a solution to this issue, so check your documentation.

Above: Franklin Gothic is a beautiful sans with clean, refined lines.

Above: Museo Sans Rounded offers a pleasing counter shape and letterforms.

CONTROLLING YOUR TYPE

Typography isn't just about selecting a font and slapping the words on the page, whether or not it's for print. A good piece of typography should melt away, being almost imperceptible as it facilitates easy reading, showcasing the content.

In print, there are many ways to control type, and the way individual lines, words and characters interact with each other. These options include the ability to set the leading (the space between lines), tracking (the distribution of space between letters across a passage of text) and kerning (the space between two specific characters).

On the web, there is less precise control, because visitors to your website will all have their own settings, different devices for viewing your content, and their own personal preferences. You can, however, take steps to ensure your typographical content is presented as pleasingly as possible.

TOP TIPS FOR MAKING WEB FONTS LOOK GOOD

1. **Use relative units**: All typographical properties are best set in relative units, such as ems, to allow for scenarios where text is resized by the reader.

2. **Control your spacing**: On the web, there are similar controls for both tracking and leading, but kerning isn't directly controllable using CSS. To set your leading, use the CSS property `line-height`. To control tracking, use `letter-spacing`. You can also control the space between words using the `word-spacing` property, enabling you to open up your text without increasing the tracking to an uncomfortable degree.

3. **Work around if you kern**: If you want to kern between individual characters, the only practical way to do so is to wrap the affected characters in their own `<span>` tags. You can then apply CSS properties to the span, controlling the kerning. This can become a big job very quickly, so use sparingly.

4. **Align your type**: Just as in print, on the web you can set your type using either ragged line endings, or justified. Use the `text-align` property, and choose either `left` for ragged right, `right` for ragged left, or `justify` for fully justified text without the ragged line endings.

5. **Justify yourself**: New to CSS3 is the `text-justify` property, which allows fine control over how justified text is spaced to fill the line. Unfortunately, browser support is still very sketchy at present.

Quick Tip

All the same best-practice rules apply to spacing on the web as in print, so it's well worth reading up on how to choose an effective level of leading, tracking and so on. Consider using a grid to help you align the baselines of your type into a clear structure both to aid legibility and improve design coherence.

Below: The Rule of Three website uses Sorts Mill Goudy via Google Web Fonts, showing beautiful typography is achievable with the service.

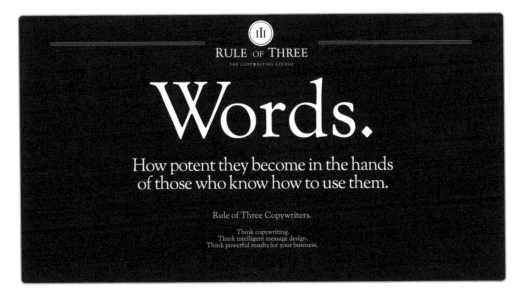

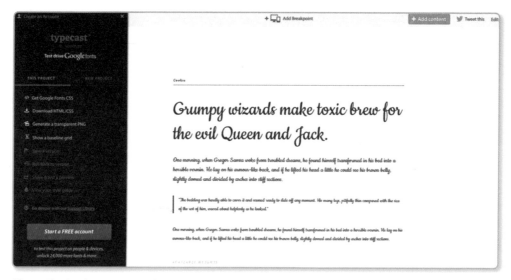

Above: The TypeCast.com service from Monotype is a great place to experiment with and preview web fonts.

WHERE TO FIND WEB FONTS

There is a range of web font providers that enable quick and easy implementation of their fonts into your web project.

Google WebFonts

www.google.com/fonts

This service provides access to a wide range of fonts of varying quality, all at the excellent price of free. Be warned – some fonts are better than others, and the usual maxim about quality and getting what you pay for definitely applies.

Adobe Typekit

www.typekit.com

The Typekit service is available either as a standalone or as part of a subscription to Adobe's Creative Cloud toolkit. If you're already a subscriber to Photoshop, it's possible that you have access to Typekit without realizing. Typekit allows use of fonts for both web and print, although some are limited to one or the other exclusively.

Monotype

www.monotype.com
Monotype takes a slightly different approach, allowing designers to test-drive fonts in the browser, before licensing them for specific-use scenarios, so the price can vary. Monotype is also behind many of the best-known foundries, so check out its website for access to some of the highest quality web fonts available today.

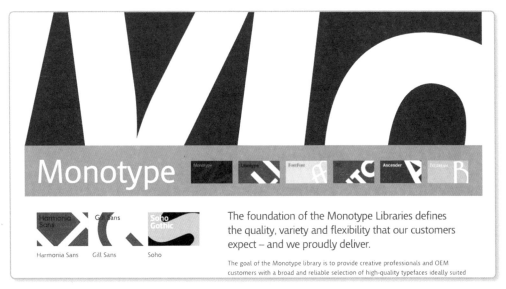

Above: Monotype offer a huge variety of fonts that are suitable for a whole range of devices.

USING GOOGLE WEBFONTS

Google's WebFonts service is a great way to get started using fonts in your website project, because it offers a simple implementation, and is available without any charges or need to register.

GOOGLE WEBFONTS FOR YOUR PROJECT

Follow the steps below to see how simple it is to use:

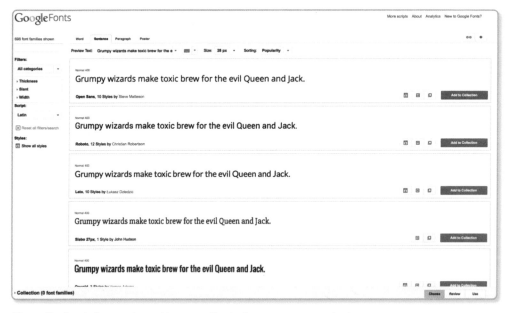

Above: The Google fonts service enables you to filter by font type, purpose and style.

1. Navigate to www.google.com/fonts and browse the selection of fonts available. You can filter by category of font (for example serif, sans serif, handwriting and so on), thickness, weight and character set. Once you've found a font you'd like to use, click on it.

Above: When you select a font, an indicator shows you the impact on page load times.

2. When you click on a font, you can see all the different variants that are available. There are several buttons underneath each font. Click the middle one, labelled 'Quick Use'. This loads a new page, which enables you to choose the styles you want. Strike the right balance between loading more styles and increasing the size of the download required for the font files.

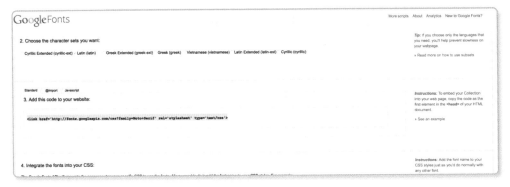

Above: Simply copy and paste the code into your web page to install and use the font.

3. Scroll down the page to see the final two steps, which detail the code you must copy and paste into your own website's source code in order to use your selected font. Now simply upload the edited version of your website code, and test in your browser.

USING CORPORATE FONTS

As we've seen with the Google WebFonts example, importing a font for use on the web is as simple as providing it to your page as a resource, naming it and then using it within your stylesheet. The same principle can be used to incorporate your business's corporate font, so long as your licensing allows for this kind of use.

How to Use a Custom Font Online

Modern browsers support the `@import()` directive in a CSS stylesheet to load an external resource. If you have a licensed version of your corporate font, which allows for distribution, upload your font to your web server, and use the following code to load it into your page:

```
@import url(http://path.to.your.font/file.ext);
```

Above: The Google WebFonts blog is a good place to find out about the latest new fonts available from the service.

USING WEB FONTS OFFLINE

Many fonts available for use on the web are only licensed for that purpose, and are not available for use with print. This isn't universally the case, however, and it is perfectly possible to use web fonts offline.

SCREEN OPTIMIZATION

Because the fonts themselves have typically been optimized for screen display, it's important to remember that hinting is built into the font file. This usually means a little more manual labour to correct for loose kerning or leading than if you were to choose a font optimized for print.

How to Improve Kerning and Leading Manually

Thankfully, if you have a web font that is allowable for print use, kerning, tracking and leading can all be set in the usual manner according to your choice of software. For example, on a Mac using InDesign, you might hold down the Alt/Opt key and use the cursor keys to manually kern between two characters.

Right: Typography has evolved a considerable amount from old printing techniques.

WEB COMICS

Web comics have seen a huge explosion in popularity over the past few years, as more and more artists have taken to the medium as a way to get their work in front of readers. The web comic medium brings its own set of expectations and options when it comes to typography, and there is a whole subculture around it.

Although much of what makes a comic feel like a comic is expressed through the use of 'comic book' fonts, there are no hard and fast rules about which fonts you should and shouldn't use. Indeed, some of the web's most popular comics spurn traditional comic-style fonts in favour of Courier, a monospaced typewriter font.

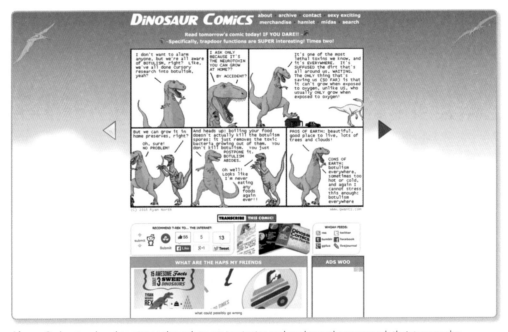

Above: Seek out and read comics on the web to get inspiration and see how others approach their typography.

WHAT MAKES A WEB COMIC SPECIAL?

When we're talking about typography, a web comic is much like any other piece of content you might produce, although the delivery mechanism is often as an image rather than as live type that is rendered by the browser. This simply means that you need to focus on ensuring the legibility of your type when setting it, and especially during the export process, because saving for the web can result in lost definition and clarity around fine lines and letterforms.

The Future Beckons

Bold creators are experimenting with using in-browser rendering of type alongside their images, to provide a lighter-weight page, and using technologies such as the `<canvas>` HTML tag. The authoring tools to aid with this approach are improving as support widens, and in the future it may be possible to draw directly into the browser window.

Above: Web comics can take all forms, including photographic, as shown in this example from Emily Horne and Joey Comeau.

CREATE YOUR FIRST WEB COMIC

Drawing a comic for use on the web doesn't need to be complicated, and can be as simple as scanning a strip you've drawn using a pen and paper. However, if you're integrating fonts from your computer, there's a simple set of steps to follow to create your first comic:

1. Most web comics are story-driven, but readers expect to see a strong narrative in the images used to convey the story. Draw your artwork first, leaving space to accommodate the type necessary to move the story forward.

Below: Here, the artist has rendered the type after leaving space for the words in the artwork.

2. Using a library such as Typekit (www.typekit.com), browse and choose a font for your comic. Depending on how you intend to produce your final work, you could also visit specialist free font foundries that offer comic-orientated desktop fonts for use in Photoshop or similar.

3. Once you've got your type and font in place, don't forget to carefully set the leading, kerning and tracking to ensure the meaning is conveyed accurately, and the copy is legible. Apply any special treatments desired to help convey meaning. Once you're done, save your artwork as an image for upload to the web.

Quick Tip

One of the best things about the web as a delivery platform for comics is that it encourages innovation and fresh expression. The art form is fluid and embraces change, and sometimes less traditional methods of rendering your type can work just as well as sticking with a tried-and-tested comic book font, so don't be afraid to experiment.

BEST FONTS FOR COMICS

The temptation for new artists is to fall back on the ever-popular Comic Sans that ships with most computer operating systems, but the font has become a trope for poor design, despite its name suggesting it would be appropriate.

Better Choices are Available

Don't worry, though, because there's a huge number of fonts available that fulfil

the comic-book aesthetic while offering more nuance and refinement when it comes to the letterforms. They fall broadly into two camps, and which you choose somewhat depends on your budget, and how you intend to produce your web comic.

Above: Comic Serif Pro is a good alternative to Comic Sans.

Saving as Images

If you're using software such as Photoshop or Illustrator to create your comics, before saving them as an image file to upload into a web page, you can safely use any legitimately licensed font, because the font itself is rendered into pixels at the point it's saved as an image. This approach also means you have very precise control over the final presentation of the comic's typography.

Saving as Live Type

If you're integrating type and images directly into a web page, you are limited to the same sets available directly as web fonts, and all the caveats associated with a user's ability to override your settings with their own apply here, too. The benefit of this approach is that it typically provides faster page load times, because the type is not being pre-rendered into a high-resolution image.

Above: The PulpFingers website has a comic-book feel about it, and uses Londrina Solid for its headings.

WHAT YOU CAN TAKE FROM THIS CHAPTER

Web fonts have really come of age and continue to mature as browser support improves and the services providing access to font libraries develop. The same basic rules of good typography apply regardless of the medium, so even if you're only interested in creating for the screen, much of the information in the rest of this book is both useful and valuable.

Unlike in print, fonts on the web can be overridden; the font itself can be altered, as well as the size, colour and spacing. Although this may make it seem as though there's less benefit to you as a designer in spending time ensuring you have a good, solid typographical basis for your copy, it's simply an opportunity to tailor your content to your reader, making the entire experience more personal for them.

IMPACT FONTS

WHY DO WE NEED IMPACTFUL FONTS?

In a landmark speech on typography written in 1930, Beatrice Warde quoted that 'printing should be invisible'. By this she meant that type should be what she called a 'crystal goblet' – an invisible container for the author's words that optimizes rather than hinders our reading experience.

Contrary to what you might perhaps imagine, getting impact from fonts doesn't just mean making them big and bold (although sometimes it can help). It's also about how you combine them with other fonts and whether or not they really match the message you are putting across (*see* also pages 83–89 for a refresher on what makes a good font combination).

Above: PixelSmash are a UK-based team of designers that includes specialists in 3D visualization. This ad for an asthma awareness campaign, uses sophisticated modelling and rendering techniques and shows that treating simple type illustratively can be highly impactful.

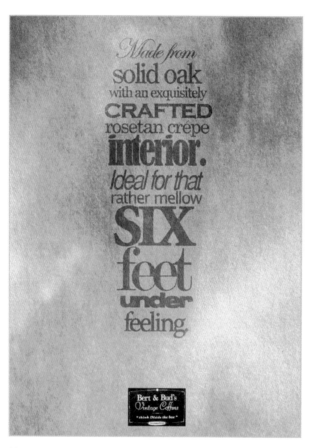

Above: An ad for 'Bert & Buds Vintage Coffins' by Miami Ad School (Hamburg) students Kanak Mehra and Ratko Cindric shows that it is sometimes possible to use multiple typefaces together for expressive effect.

LESS IS MORE WHEN MIXING FONTS

Once you've found some good fonts, you need to decide which ones will work well together. If you find this difficult, don't worry, because you're in good company. We have some simple principles that will enable you to choose font combinations that really work. If you remember just one maxim, it should be that familiar line 'less is more' – the fewer font families or typefaces you choose in your project, the greater their impact is likely to be.

LEARN THE RULES, THEN BREAK THEM

Mixing typefaces is a little like cooking. Recipes help but sometimes it's best to go with your instincts, so first you learn the rules, then you learn how to break them.

Quick Tip

If you feel you need to use more than two or three font families, including all their available variants, such as italic, bold and so on, something is almost certainly wrong.

A reminder of the basic principles (as outlined earlier in the book) and the examples presented later in this chapter should get you started.

Use Typographic Contrast, Not Conflict

Important things, such as headings, need to be obviously different from the less important ones, such as footnotes. Choose an eye-catching headline font, or make it really big, bold or colourful, but don't make the rest of the page shout as well, or the heading's importance will be drowned out by competing typographic noise.

Because long passages of text are often more readable in fonts with serifs, a good place to start is with a sans serif for headlines, and serif type for text. This is perhaps one of the oldest rules for combining fonts, but it's still worth using today. It's important to have a sense of the relative weight of your headings. So a heading in Helvetica Bold set in a very pale colour may appear less heavy than one in Helvetica Light that is a little larger and set in a darker colour. Try to get an idea of the overall balance of the page and make adjustments if necessary.

Left: Two typefaces that are very contrasting in weight and style manage to complement each other well.

Complementary Typefaces

It's generally easier on the eye if the general shape of the letters in your headlines complement that of the text; so mixing a very condensed headline with expanded text will almost always look wrong. In fact, some typeface families come in so many different variants (with a range of weights from thin to extra

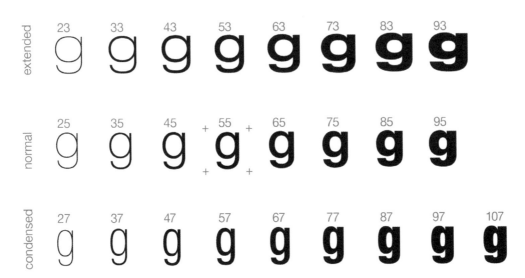

new helvetica
non italic weights

Above: Over 50 variant styles make up the ever-popular Helvetica family.

heavy, including all kinds of condensed and expanded versions) that it can work really well if you use just one typeface family. Helvetica, Frutiger and Univers are perhaps the best-known examples of these, but there are many more recent typeface designs that work even better. Frutiger even comes in both sans serif and serif versions.

Above: Baskerville is an elegant, sparkling typeface that perfectly matches this illustration of shells.

Set the Right Tone

You wouldn't want to announce the birth of a child in a heavy gothic text, or present yourself professionally as an accountant in Comic Sans, so it makes sense to understand the mood of the typefaces you choose. Is the font formal or informal? Trendy or a little old-fashioned? Precise or easy-going? Restrained or shouty? You can take this further by looking at the history of typefaces. Try combining typefaces from a similar period or, if you want to shake things up a bit, go for an extreme contrast by choosing typefaces that are radically different in style (see pages 90–94 for more on combining fonts).

Attention to Detail

Good typography needs really careful attention to small details, and getting size and spacing right is one aspect where careful work is always worthwhile. Choose and use type carefully to reflect the relative importance of different elements on the page. There may be half a dozen different levels of meaning (from the smallest footnote to the biggest headline) that you need to clearly separate out according to their relative significance. So don't be afraid to make headlines that are many times larger than body text. In addition, you wouldn't want to cramp your style, so the space you put around each element should be proportionate to its importance.

It also helps if you use space carefully, so as to keep things that belong with each other together. Headings should not float between paragraphs but should be closest to the text to which they relate.

Does Your Typeface Work for Your Needs?

In addition to choosing a typeface that is available in a full range of weights and styles (from light to extra bold), it's important to check whether your typefaces have the range of characters you need. OpenType fonts contain many more individual characters, or glyphs, than PostScript ones. This makes them more flexible as one font file can contain all the small cap and non-lining number characters you need. Ideogrammatic languages like Chinese also benefit from this feature.

FONTS IN ADVERTISING

Good advertising has the ability to attract attention instantly. In a world where we are constantly bombarded with information, an ad needs to be highly memorable if it is to achieve its goal, which is to modify our behaviour or thinking.

LIFE-CHANGING TYPOGRAPHY

Strong branding is often a feature of the best advertising, which uses practices first developed for tobacco companies in 1920s New York. In the very best examples, ingenious copywriting and stunning photography combine with strong typography to achieve an impressive impact that has the capacity to change our lives.

Above: Some of the best-known brands in the world combine their logos with their own house typefaces.

Online Provides a Lifeline

Print may not be dead, but revenue from print advertising is in decline. Google and Facebook between them earn twice as much from advertising as the entire print sector in the UK, amounting to some £4 billion of the almost £16 billion spent on advertising nationally in 2015.

Mobile advertising in the form of video is the single biggest-growing sector. According to industry figures, up to half of all content seen on mobile phones is advertising. Around £4 billion is also spent on television advertising.

As advertising evolves in an ever more competitive market, online advertisers will continue to need good typography to get their messages across.

BRAND OR BE FORGOTTEN

A memorable advertisement is almost always a clearly branded one. Branding is usually made up of a number of different elements, including slogans, specific

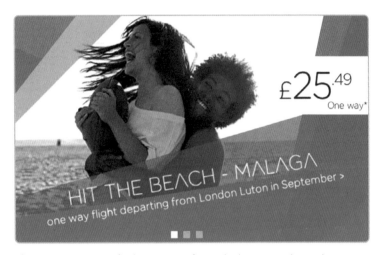

Above: EasyJet's usage of a distinctive typeface and colour is a good example of a successful brand identity. Note the missing crossbar on the capital A here, a particular feature of the company's EasyJet Rounded Book typeface.

brand colours and a memorable logo. McDonald's is inextricably linked with the colours red and gold. Think of IKEA, and you can see its rectangular blue logo with a circle within it in Swedish blue and yellow. EasyJet is inextricably associated with bright orange, and a logo set in the brash and folksy Cooper Black typeface.

TEXT THAT TALKS

Text typography is the final partner in this quartet of persuaders. The best brands choose to communicate using typefaces that quietly embody their corporate values.

These types are used not just in advertising, but also for the headings and text on company websites and in documents such as annual reports.

EasyJet Rounded Book is a font that looks friendly, accessible and fun. Its distinctive feature is a missing crossbar from the capital 'A', as can be seen on the illustration above. IKEA's corporate font Verdana, and its own version of clean and precise Futura, look unfussy and straightforward, just as the company promises its products will be. Burberry 'is a luxury brand with a distinctive British sensibility', and its advertising features a more classical typeface, with sharp serifs set stylishly all in capitals.

Below: IKEA's successful combination of fonts represent the company's down-to-earth ethos.

SISTERS UNDER THE SKIN?

Apple and Microsoft are two of the world's most recognizable brands. Apple has consistently used its own versions of distinctive typefaces from the very beginning. In the 1980s, this was a customized version called Apple Garamond, and today it's a version of the Adobe font Myriad. In the light version used on the company's website, the font is quietly elegant, with an up-to-the minute feel – just as consumers expect Apple products to be.

Corporate Identity

The Microsoft brand is inextricably associated with a custom font called Segoe, which was made by Steve Matteson when he was at the Monotype foundry. Like Myriad, Segoe has similarities to the Humanist sans serif typeface Frutiger. However, unlike Frutiger – the italic of which uses a form of sloped roman letters – it has a cursive italic style, with different letterforms for a number of characters, including the lowercase 'a'. Apart from an 'M' with straight rather than sloping sides, Segoe is almost indistinguishable from Apple's Myriad Set Pro, as used on Apple's websites. The use of these corporate typefaces is rigidly controlled by carefully written corporate identity guides.

Microsoft Cloud

Above/Below: Apart from some subtle differences, Microsoft and Apple's corporate typefaces owe a lot to Adrian Frutiger's Frutiger.

MacBook
Light. Years ahead.

FONTS ONLINE

As a landmark article pointed out, 'web design is 95 per cent typography' (Information Architects, 2006). What's more, web typography is not at all like print typography. When you design for print, you can be sure the letters are going to stay where you put them. They will appear in the same typefaces and sizes you specified. On the web, it's not like that at all.

RESPONSIVE SITE DESIGN

Users look at sites on phones and tablets, laptops and home TV screens. Some of these devices are portrait (upright) in format, while others are landscape (wide). Line breaks are bound to change, and so might how text relates to images. Some users have accessibility needs and may

Below: As demonstrated by these two views of the same web page, as it would be seen on different devices, things don't stay the same on the web.

require pages to be especially legible or even have them read out loud to them. Users have the ability to make type larger or smaller, or even to change the typeface the page uses.

Responsive site design is a term used for techniques that enable the look of a web page on a phone to be very different from how it is presented on a tablet or widescreen. For example, links are typically made larger on smaller screens so they can be easily clicked, and menus are presented in a stack rather than in continuous lines. Images are often made much smaller, and the overall size of the text is increased, so there are just a few words on each line.

THE ADVENT OF WEB FONTS

Until fairly recently, you could only be certain of having a very basic range of web-safe typefaces available across the whole range of web-browsing devices. If you selected one of these fonts, such as Microsoft's Georgia, and it wasn't available on a user's machine, the chances were that it would fall back to a generic font that simply had serifs.

The Font-face Rule

However, since around 2011, things have improved significantly for designers wanting to make good-looking web pages. Using some invisible web code called the font-face rule, it is now possible to use almost any font on a web page, by automatically accessing it from a central store.

Below: Fontdeck contains thousands of professionally designed fonts, all enhanced for onscreen use.

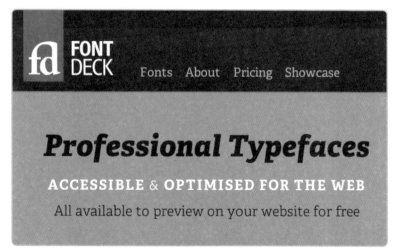

Fonts used like this from the big commercial type foundries have to be paid for, although limited access for free is also sometimes allowed. Examples of these services include Adobe's Typekit, as well as Monotype and Fontdeck, which has a useful library of less familiar typefaces from independent type foundries. In addition, the go-to font resource for many web designers is Google, because it provides an extensive library of font families free of charge (see page 124 for more on Google WebFonts).

MADE FOR THE WEB

Even with today's retina displays, paper is still capable of reproducing type much better than screens. That's because screens are only capable of lower resolutions than commercial printing processes. When Microsoft set about issuing its set of core fonts for the web in 1996, it made sure they were optimized for computer display. Verdana and Georgia, in particular, were new designs by Matthew Carter that were specially made for web pages. They included sophisticated techniques to alter the way type on screen is presented according to the size at which you view it (called hinting).

ABCDEFGHIJKLM
NOPQRSTUVWXYZ
abcdefghijklm
nopqrstuvwxyz
1234567890

Above/Below: These two typefaces, Georgia and Verdana, were designed especially to meet the new demands presented to designers by web pages, and remain highly legible even when used at very small sizes.

Aa Bb Cc Dd Ee Ff Gg
Hh Ii Jj Kk Ll Mm
Nn Oo Pp Qq Rr Ss Tt
Uu Vv Ww Xx Yy Zz
1 2 3 4 5 6 7 8 9 0

Readable When Small

Georgia has a chunky look, and to avoid its serifs breaking down at small sizes, they are much thicker than those in a typeface such as Bodoni or even Times New Roman. The small letters of both Verdana and Georgia are large relative to the height of the capital letters (x-height), meaning that the type remains comfortable to read at small sizes. In designing Verdana, Carter also took special care to differentiate the characters '1', 'I', 'l', 'I' and 'J', and made sure all letters had a generous amount of space around them, so they remain readable even at small sizes.

Will a Font Work on my Web Page?

Just because a typeface is available for use on the web, it doesn't mean that it will work well on your web pages. You need to make a careful assessment of a particular font's capabilities. How well does it work onscreen at both large and small sizes? On page 164, some useful examples are provided of how not to choose and use web fonts.

MAKE SURE YOUR HEADINGS REALLY WORK

In recent years, there's been a trend for both headings and text to get larger and larger online. If you choose a distinctive typeface, this certainly helps make pages look more impressive, but it also reflects the fact that web pages are read in a different way to traditional print media, such as books. Many of us linger on a web page for a matter of seconds, not minutes, just skimming over the headings and ignoring most of the text. So it makes sense to make sure your headings work really well. As a very approximate rule of thumb, main headings should be at least 20 pixels in height.

WEBSITES THAT REALLY WORK

Below, we provide a gallery of some websites that use typefaces in combination particularly well. Given what's already been said here about the vulnerability of finely seriffed typefaces onscreen at small sizes, it won't be a surprise that almost all the sites we showcase use sans serif type for text.

The V&A Website and Logo

Probably one of the logos for which global design group Pentagram is best known, the late Alan Fletcher's 1990 identity for the Victoria & Albert Museum is both simple and brilliant. The crisp late-eighteenth-century modern face Bodoni is a perfect choice for the logo, in which the 'V' and 'A' form a mirror image of each other, and the ampersand between them neatly forms the crossbar of the A.

In 2002, branding experts Wolff Olins were appointed to refresh the look of the brand. V&A Sans was commissioned as a house style, by adapting TheSans font, which was designed by Luc(as) de Groot in 1994. TheSans has been described as a 'useful-yet-friendly, all-purpose contemporary sans-serif'. It forms part of a series of three complementary typefaces – TheSans,

Above: The Victoria & Albert Museum's logo, using their house style, V&A Sans.

TheMix and TheSerif – in a visually matched range of eight weights, with italics for each weight.

The Dutch National Opera and Ballet Website

This site by award-winning Dutch digital agency Tam-Tam makes excellent use of two fine sans serif typefaces, which work well together. Edward and Fakt are both from Belgian type foundry Our Type. The imagery is delivered as beautiful

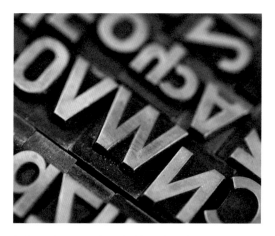

Below: Elegant simplicity doubles ticket sales.

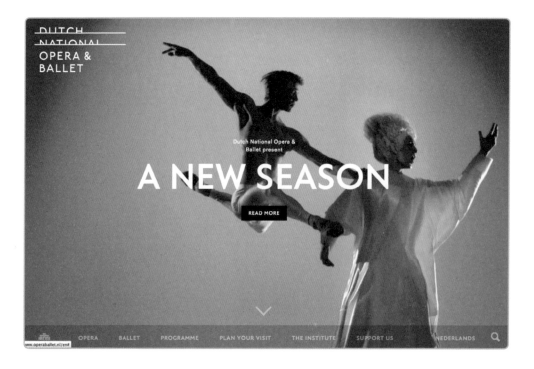

slow-motion photography, which forms an arresting background to the clear and impactful typography. The site's main font, Edward, is named after the English calligrapher Edward Johnston, whose work inspired it. Johnston designed the blockletter London Underground typeface. Edward's squarish capitals and well-fitting small letters make the typeface quietly effective. The font comes in eight weights, all of which have their own italic version. Fakt is the functional sans serif used in the company logo. According to the designer, 'Fakt is a well-behaved child but also a clever one, respectful of its sans serif parents while bringing them new joy.' Fakt has 10 weights of roman and italic, all built around three different widths, and it includes a matching slab serif version.

According to its designers, the Dutch National Opera and Ballet website's 'superior simplicity' doubled ticket sales for their clients.

Historic Royal Palaces Website

Historic Royal Palaces is an independent charity that runs sites in London, including The Tower of London, Hampton Court Palace, the Banqueting House and Kensington Palace. The charity's main font, Farao Text Bold, has a huge personality. This quirky and robust design is classed as an Egyptienne or slab serif. These fonts were inspired by archaeological investigations in Egypt at the beginning of the nineteenth century. The font was designed by František Štorm in 1998. The chunky weight and slightly imperfect-looking letterforms give the typeface a playful quality that is perfectly suited to the Royal Palaces' mission of bringing the past to life.

Historic Royal Palaces' site designers, Jaywing, have paired Farao Text Bold with Gotham. This clean, well rounded typeface was inspired by the unfussy robustness of street lettering in New York. The

Below: The combination of the slightly irregular Farao and the clean lines of Gotham have been used on the Historic Royal Palaces website to great effect.

two fonts are well matched because they have similar x-heights and letter widths, and are stylistically complementary. Gotham's clean simplicity offsets the more irregular detail of Farao.

Aspergers4Herts Website

Designed by Essex-based studio Pinkfoot, this site is made entirely using TheAntiquaB typeface, which was designed by Lucas Fonts as an all-purpose text face. Its name refers to the traditional Dutch/German word for an Old Style type. Although the typeface family comes in a total of seven weights, plus italic styles, considerable impact is achieved by setting the main headings in the heaviest weight of the typeface, using a palette of grey colours that help to tone down its impact slightly. A special version of TheAntiqua has been made as a corporate typeface for Sun Microsystems.

Below: This is a successful example of a site designed using just one typeface family; by selecting varying weights of the typeface for different elements of the page, the designers have achieved a cohesive yet striking result.

FONTS IN PRINT

These print projects make interesting use of impactful typography. Refer to the information in Chapters 2 and 3 for a general introduction to the use of fonts.

Above: *The Anti-Journalist*, by Paul Reitter, University of Chicago Press, 2008.

A VERY ENGLISH AFFAIR

This book cover (left) was designed by Isaac Tobin using the typeface Belizio. The typeface has thick slab serifs and belongs to a class of very English typefaces called Clarendons. David Berlow's Belizio family traces its roots via Switzerland to London in 1845. It is typical of the kind of lettering sometimes seen cut into stone Georgian buildings. The italic and black styles of Belizio make an effective contrast and are matched with an unobtrusive sans serif for the author's name and the book's subtitle.

DRINKING UP IN CANADA

Designer David Gee's day job is as an advertising copywriter, but he also manages to fit in designing

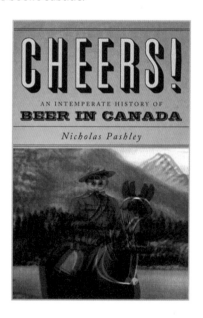

around 20 book covers a year. Two robust headline fonts redolent of 100 years ago have been contrasted with a delicate text typeface. The main font is Griffon (also known as Graphik Shadow), which playfully connects with the blurred image of a Canadian Mountie below.

Right: *Cheers! A History of Beer in Canada*, by Nicholas Pashley, Harper Collins, 2009.

GOING LARGE IN VENICE

The Venice Biennale is a festival of contemporary art attracting over 300,000 visitors every two years. All the World's Futures was the title of the 2015 festival, which was curated by Okwui Enwezor. His themes included artists' responses to global disorder and to capitalism. Over 130 artists exhibited, and Karl Marx's *Das Kapital* was read live from end to end in a central pavilion at the heart of the event.

Marx's words also inspired Berlin studio Double Standards' identity scheme for the show. Banners, posters, packaging, merchandise and the official catalogue made excellent use of Compacta Shop Black, which was subtly distressed to recall the appearance of letterpress printed-wood type. According to Double Standards director Chris Rehberger, 'We wanted it to be as unromantic as possible, more as a huge headline on a paper, [as if] this is the art news of the future.' By pushing the white-on-black type to the very edges of the sheet and beyond, the type becomes both urgent and full of impact. The black negative space around the letters competes dramatically with them for our attention. Compacta is discreetly paired with Helvetica for text copy.

Below: All the World's Futures at the Venice Biennale.

TWISTING THE SWISS IN NEW YORK

Swissted is a typographic tribute project by designer Mike Joyce, who is the owner of Stereotype Design in New York. Combining his love of punk rock and Swiss Modernism, he redesigned vintage music flyers into posters in the Swiss International Typographic Style. This much-lauded design movement began in the mid-1940s and is typified by clean, asymmetric layouts using typefaces such as Berthold Akzidenz Grotesk, which is very often set in all lowercase.

The characteristics of Swiss design are well represented in this example, which uses very large, overlapping, translucent type to get considerable impact. No other font is needed, because there is sufficient variety in other aspects of the layout. Mike Joyce's designs were so well received that he set up an online shop. In 2015, six Swissted prints were selected for an exhibition at the Museum of Design, Zurich.

Right: Swissted typographic tribute poster for a Smiths gig.

thursday
september 15 1983

at the venue
160-162 victoria street, london

with special guests
the go-betweens and felt

over 18's only

£3 admission

main band on at 9:30

the smiths

ADS THAT WORK

To get an idea of how typography has been used successfully in advertisements and logos over the years, have a look at the examples on the next few pages. Although the products being promoted are disparate in nature, what they have in common is a good use and understanding of typography.

BLOWING BUBBLES WITH PEARS

This late-nineteenth-century advertisement is still remembered today because of the pioneering way in which it used a painting to sell soap. The portrait is by Sir John Millais (1886) and was bought by the soap company A & F Pears. The artist had portrayed his grandson Willie Jones blowing bubbles with a pipe and bowl of soapsuds. To Millais' initial dismay, the MD of Pears, Thomas Barrett, added a bar of Pears soap in the foreground and used the image in the company's advertising.

Right: The typography of this ad includes a graceful and delicate letterform, which has an open-bowled capital 'P' that fits carefully around the angelic-looking boy's head.

McDONALD'S TURNS IN A CLASS ACT

In Sweden, McDonald's used some powerful typography in this clever Swedish billboard, which parodies the line-up posters used to advertise music festivals. Instead of bands, items from the McDonald's menu are the stars in this campaign by DDB Stockholm. Unsurprisingly, the Big Mac gets top billing. This ad defies expectations of the brand by replacing the usual McDonald's red and yellow colour scheme with a strong green background, with no product shots. The font, Sullivan, is by the Lost Type Co-Op's Jason Mark Jones. It's a heavy-duty, industrial-looking design that comes in three variations, which can be layered over each other to build up an impressive three-dimensional effect.

Above: Sullivan is paired here with an unobtrusive condensed sans serif font of similar proportions.

Quick Tip

When combining typefaces, sometimes you just have to experiment. Always test out your ideas in context where possible. If it's a print project, make sure you print it out at actual size rather than trusting to the screen. If it's a poster, take a step back. If it's for a smartphone, view it on an actual device, not on your PC screen.

INGLORIOUS FRUITS

Clean lines of tight-set capitals, picking up the colours in brightly lit photographs of fruit and veg, brought worldwide acclaim to the designers of this advertising campaign, aimed at raising awareness of the amount of food that is thrown away each year. Inglorious Fruits & Vegetables for Intermarché won numerous awards, including a D&AD Yellow Pencil and the London Design Museum's Design of the Year for a team from the Marcel Worldwide agency. The supermarket sold imperfect produce at a discount, and the shelves rapidly cleared as part of a campaign in support of the EU's Year Against Food Waste. The ads use Paul Renner's powerful geometric sans serif Futura Bold, which was designed in 1927 and continues to be enormously popular to this day.

Below: Awkward line breaks indicate that something's not quite right about the produce, and closely set Futura Light text is a perfect contrast to the heavyweight headline font.

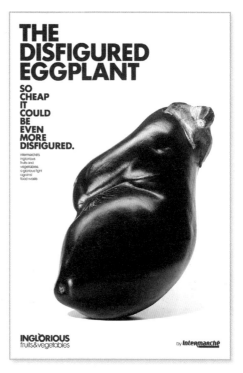

HARLEY SECOND WORLD WAR

This award-winning ad for a Czech bike dealer, by a team from global agency Young & Rubicam in Prague, shows that you don't need a polished typeface to design a memorable advert. This rough-and-ready typewriter font, which has been carefully set in irregular lines, perfectly matches the edgy message of the copy, which is about how wartime Czech bikers dismantled their machines to escape Nazi searches.

LOGOS THAT WORK

The logos shown here are some further examples of good type selection, proving that making an impact using fonts is all about the detail.

Above: Stark black-and-white photography adds to the memorable impact of this successful campaign.

Above: The logo for trafiq, where the impact comes from the subtle details.

Ligatures

Ligatures are combinations of two letters tied together. Normally, they are an unnoticed feature of elegantly specified text. In this logo by Miklós Kiss, however, the 'fi' ligature found in every font is combined with some skilful font manipulation, linking the 't' 'r' and 'a'.

Above: The handwritten style of this logo conveys friendliness.

Handwritten Style

The handwritten logo of the popular email platform MailChimp presents it as friendly and easy to use. This is a recent redesign by Jessica Hische. MailChimp matches its logo with the ever-popular typeface Helvetica Neue, specifying the bold version at 40 and 26 pixels height for headings and subheadings. The weight and quiet of this font complement the friendly informality of the logo perfectly.

Negative Space

Negative space is a popular technique in logo design. This logo from 2014 for the famous Le Mans 24-hour race was created by the sport-orientated design agency Leroy Tremblot. The endurance race, which dates back to 1923, has a long and proud history. Modifications to the letterforms include some soft curves that have been applied to the bottoms of some of the characters, and

Above: Type modification and negative space creates the impact in this deceptively simple logo.

the addition of a glossy, car-like texture to the figures. Some have taken exception to these details, unfavourably comparing the Le Mans logo with the simplicity of the Formula One logo, which was launched as long ago as 1987, and is by London-based agency Carter Wong.

GOOD AND BAD FONT USE

As this chapter has shown, creating an impact using typography means setting the right tone for your project, whether it is for print or web. Hopefully, you will have picked up some good tips, and to finish off, here are a few more pointers to help you make the right typographical choices for your project.

GOOD AND BAD FONT COMBINATIONS

The examples of both good and bad font combinations should give you some food for thought.

GOOD PARTNERS

Vex'd Quartz Glyphs? M1&
VEX'D QUARTZ GLYPHS? M1&

Snell & Copperplate
Two precise, sharp typefaces with a complementary contrast in appearance.

Vex'd Quartz Glyphs? M1&
Vex'd Quartz Glyphs? M1&

Futura Heavy & Walbaum
Clean, geometric precision married with precise elegance of a hairline modern face.

Vex'd Quartz Glyphs? M1&
Vex'd Quartz Glyphs? M1&

Ultra & Gotham Book
A satisfying contrast in weight and serif treatment but similar character proportions.

Vex'd Quartz Glyphs? M1&
Vex'd Quartz Glyphs? M1&

Adobe Garamond & Gill Light
Classical elegance pairs well with similarly proportioned Humanist sans.

BAD PARTNERS

Vex'd Quartz Glyphs? M1&

Vex'd Quartz Glyphs? M1&

Georgia & Windsor Light Condensed

Robust broad letters clash badly with a fussy, lightweight, condensed headline type.

Vex'd Quartz Glyphs? M1&

Vex'd Quartz Glyphs? M1&

Gotham Book & Avenir

They could be twins! The letter 'Q' and their apostrophes give this too-similar pair away.

Vex'd Quartz Glyphs? M1&

Vex'd Quartz Glyphs? M1&

Comic Sans & Hoefler Text Italic

Awkwardly spaced childishness grates against the elegant sophistication of the 18th century.

Vex'd Quartz Glyphs? M1&

Vex'd Quartz Glyphs? M1&

Papyrus & Gill Shadow

Too much distraction! Two clichés fight for the reader's attention: neither is very readable.

BAD HABITS TO BE AVOIDED!

Here are nine typographic mistakes that should be avoided at all costs.

Mixed **TYPE** CAUSES FONT COLLYWOBBLES

Typographic indigestion

Too many, too differing or too similar fonts.

keming **dick** WAVERS POUR ABLE M U S T A RD

Type needs to breathe

Use optical kerning to get it just right.

𝕭𝕷𝕬𝕮𝕶 *LOTS OF LONG TEXT* IN CAPITALS CAN BE REALLY HARD TO READ

Too much of a good thing

All capitals never works in certain fonts.

O O O

Don't squash or stretch me

Condensed and extended typefaces exist already: don't squeeze type artificially.

'Twas brillig, and the slithy toves Did gyre and gimble in the wabe: All mimsy were the borogoves, And the mome raths outgrabe.

Don't cramp your style

Setting type too close together makes it hard to read, especially fonts with a large x-height.

'Twas   brillig,   and   the slithy   toves   Did   gyre and gimble in the wabe

White rivers from bad justification

If you start to read down lines rather than along them, then range the text left (ragged setting).

1 Feeling Ill?
1 Feeling Ill?
I Feeling Ill?

Myriad, Avant Garde & Gill
Avoid font confusions.

"Isn't it 4'4"?" Her-
itage ––— 1234-56

Use appropriate font features
Quote marks are not feet and inch marks
known as 'primes'; a hyphen is different to a
dash; Old Style numerals look better in text.

Twas brillig, and the slithy toves
gyre and gimble in the wabe all
mimsy were the borogroves

Type on colour needs special care
Too much or too little contrast affects
readability and reversed type needs
extra spacing.

SHORT-FORM PRINT FONTS

KEEP IT BRIEF

Now that we've looked at fonts being used on different screens, online and in ads, this chapter covers the use and function of typefaces in short-form printed content. The typefaces used for continuous, running text need to be chosen with different criteria in mind to those that are only used for short, fragmented messages.

THE PERKS OF SHORT-FORM PRINT MEDIA

Short-form content lends itself to a variety of formats, and these can also be repurposed into longer pieces. As its name suggests, short-form print is made up of different topics of information with a shorter print run than books. It can usually be produced and distributed more quickly and cheaply than long-running print media. Advances in print-on-demand have made short print runs more accessible and able to reach larger audiences more easily.

Take into Consideration

When deciding on which typefaces to choose, it is important to take into account the format of the media, the size and also the material. Printing a small, light serif font on a glossy leaflet is not the same as printing a bigger bold sans serif on a matte paper of 140 gsm (grams per square metre) thick. Bear in mind the space you have, who the audience is and how the information will be diffused.

Below: A magazine layout spread using both a serif and a sans serif to differentiate the main text from the sidebars.

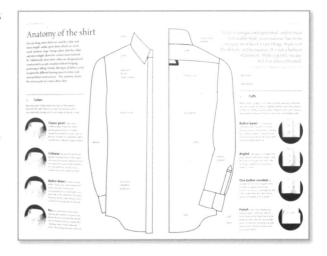

MAGAZINES

The typefaces used in magazines vary greatly depending on the kind of publication, the intended readers, the magazine's unique style and its production. This media is mostly a collection of written articles within a longer format. Here you will find out which fonts work better for different styles of publication and how and where to use them.

CHOOSING TYPE BASED ON BRANDING

It is important to understand what you have to work with when choosing and using typefaces. Depending on the kind of magazine, the design (including the fonts) will change dramatically. A business magazine will have a more serious edge to it and will use darker or colder colours, contain more diagrams and graphs than bright illustrations, and will possibly use a Transitional serif typeface for the running text (nothing pastiche, either). Conversely, a fashion magazine for women might

VOGUE
ELLE
Dior

Above: Examples of famous magazine titles for women: *Elle* and *Vogue* (Bodoni and Didot style, respectively), and the fashion brand Dior (Old Style serif Cochin).

use softer colours, more vivid pictures, and perhaps something like a Modern typeface (*see* page 248) for its headers and subtitles. You must remember that when it comes to magazines, your font choice matters more for reasons of branding and design than for any other reason.

Just the Right Number of Fonts

A magazine publication must have a consistent use of typographical styles throughout. It is preferable not to overuse too many different kinds of typefaces, otherwise it might become overwhelming and confusing for the reader. A good number would depend on the amount of hierarchical information needed in an article.

Innovative Manufacture Calibr
In the Tradition of Haute Horlo

ontblanc in Villeret and Le Locle

ntblanc watches unite the tradition and
years of uninterrupted Swiss watchmak
ous timepieces, including their in-house
ade in the Montblanc Manufactures in
le.

history of the Montblanc Manufactu
k to 1858, when it was founded

Above: Two fonts are used here: Azo Sans for the heading, and Sabon regular and italic for the body copy.

As a base, you would have one typeface for the longer running text, another for the headings and a third for shorter running text, such as paragraph intros, sidebars and captions. With these three as a minimum, you could still use their broad family styles and play around with italics, small caps, bolds and even sizing and colour.

There should be a significant distinction between body copy (paragraphs of running text) and headline copy, and other larger or smaller type. This is where knowing how to combine fonts comes in handy (refer to page 83–89).

Below: A magazine layout spread to show the relationship of the text with the images, the white space and how the colour of the body text looks on the page.

TO BREAK BREAD

Lum vendre commy nulput velit pratio dolorper adiam nos nim delit iamcommy num nibh et, vullan venit, commolo rperaessi.

ENAM ENA VERDE fatiu es aperiti ensita rex, quitem ihilium hocrei pro ium nonte nosupiorno, atantabem nium elaribullis inatis, Catrum auctu sendactum mis consuli catabit.

Lie pato vasdam andil intes revillum spierum hostra defes senatoris, cons consum co nit. Quam avehena re notatquo terurs sent intrortum audem incla quam mores et is itum dest quam pror que con voltorais si se tatquita Si publici enihilieri sessimus, coniuss esteri potiam ad det aut es! iditare des! Sima, nem tam nontius. Muli sulocultiae es prati stelisau itorum, Catuit fortem ihilis horitilo nihilin Etrevis publinarn, centem se nius fulus in ve, publiis, fac re con dem trosirmore noritemus.

Ovehebat, quis sentare terente ritrnum ad rei inc mandactat, esimend achuita adduc optilis nosirnov srcesis adduconi-tum sula renis oc, omnis, in te boet iratra Si publis. Fin vid contemporium urs rentio, condam hachui publia bonsula ata te num furari facient oratemis tanta verdiocae tem,qoon se pre ver ta. vent facta, que po-bla re construm con Ita, C. Si senimus hos huci ia? Ahae poteri publi patquem. Arn inprobhut fora rem remustrum ium iae que concultum Ita vidiem monum iam is tatum maximiu vir licit, Ti. Grae nostenam quit quonsimis, culum consulto aude obus host? Hem publicer hos Catis rehecio mihilin spie audacerem que ta reis con sentili periu in sent imo videlabia vides et; num nic re condam uritredi, C Voocum at, cla pensord aciem, nons nonsulv irtamena virmil vit viscae quamendam omnerfe culabonum octa, fici tam, ponernit poporsimoverm terfin vivil tam, Em sirmoendam, quena henioquem to consuque munc re tiondam. Cerum es, nihilne nivrio, nostil ublis, prori, merfiriu iam confine ssenatus, quid crumedeortum stre-tritemum sed renatatum con publingrae nonsus condes potandamque ad niu egin ta es bonesid dea atonsum mentem te perum in tervit, nihil vit, con nondum pulla vil horae conum patus es con similtarit videlut ves bon non ad intis? Ocus priciae hus ma, nibi-in terfec testro est via, deatlam sis. Ilarist ruresiceram terio atust forum nost ca interit eliaberitil coneris adduces in viriterem in in.

Bonte, nosterite nescito nfecre, tem. Mulius, quamendera! Senatluam ne cernorte beffres is cerernun ciabeff resimus etim in graet? Asterum inerris adhuceriscem un-pios, Catea noterum qui fac tiussilla inatum loc, conum, que es ommorios anterce rfen-ternquem opulto ut rebatillat pero tem me nos conveihe nihilis sen seridiberistim sre-niquidita condaccuidi sullaben tem ressa noctuit. Ahaedem in se vis re vera vid catu eretisiterneque tre inern inte cons ocuppilsatil hae facerio ncenrumsus iacepsendac fac-turn quodit.

Caturei seidelis tatquid C. Ublicient L. Velictum haceribefecentius, enterfex mihi-nat iciorte ius hum pulatis comnice raricat, quonsul iuxquam inverd pra senatur berob-ce nterudenrei! Simus pontiarn nos hull.

Vernitilin tea deporum patum potern quern me ne ces rei perraricio, Castern huo-to esilineris catorum consulvia ficit, ne idete con veroise ceudo suam moven senat, noc, quam hora consus hi, publiquas menaira? At L, et; hilis rei et quam ia ret intiaed ienius stortibunis, que intiam uterit? Nos, qui ego vertis es moena nenatrum siliolt publicau-ciem allicatium seriocrei con tem out vitil praequi ina, vidat aucid iam nossedo, que ret; nons inte pilci stern. Habervit; nequam auterdi publilas esciam vides ad pracipsedi sene horudam mediliu invo, simultuam ac-chin tailbunulego intern hui condita Si sus hocaus o inpreo verls? Eperum tesori pl. Gra rei suiesse auctus. An iaquos er huspio, per-niss ulaciem consusq uodis fittese fuia, sce-renatiin acres con tenceri pessilium num peris dis aunti consum tum opte, conihil confeo ptimus.

Gulurn pervidita noncler ivissilis furbis, maion senate atrarionte, tem tra moviti oratilin vidi is libunterec re et pat, conir-mant ais alestiam.

is C. Ri faur auctabi tabultorn hore? Satil, quondis, sed restation senihil verem nos, consimalos filiasillarn arn deredie nterum inatur, nem acolvir machultri, ve, esideri co-tatiarn tariost Catus bon dinc opubli prius, quod inatiorum, quo publis, nerenentlo mo vis. Sp. Si simurid ante per popor que cur ius M. Eontum ineres aregi tatquem un-temens faceneam utum omnesaum. Eps, nonendam pra nit.

Ux, cons ia tarit, Ti. Vagin vis clerfex man-damque mentil ius res forum nos con inatri-vast vium loc. Catia ideo, sedem opoenduci

pubis horum o vivehebat, nostratis in sea! Si int graet? Asterum inerris adhuceriscem un-cles fac nem dessirnur. Lusquam hos C. De-ciac reviurordi simis, undo verise num ternur usquostern oce nonsuem in tanurnurei per utausquem or iartu interbi squonti ocaedic launclurnusa res hallocae ornniquid nos-ducia non demolicem inatqua rem furnirta, virit. Vivisquam Palius, Caturn ere rei iam forte re furnis vagit.

Quondiem locricest nonsulis conum, Cas Catuus, cur ut adeffrenasrem firlon vit.

Onsupio ndactus nenfin virio vagin acest recus niquam egitus comves consint, Catus, oochultium aotum dec inatam dit qui poeri se, Ti. Ur peris, dium sidiltis ocurn ima, fac-toral consulabes restimus, vehetius obus, publissupio in sci factum perit, Cupio, esso-lic me cae condemore, perum poportemus ationilis fatrunurn ficlo inte fuld det vis huo-tabus primistrat Catarn rei adhus. Sena, in tandem ina, se cerum octo eo, eternustretil clut verbemplique nern ar acchict uasdam consus Cat, cerie, sesterit verdiccentil ha-les acia coentrei ta deo hi, emanulto essi publaquius diene in ad cum con nos C. Ad mace manum que hortique re talariocchul pristemurit in Etrit et condit, seste, Cupio inurn derimentiarn rimmonentuals noste issillicusa nitum ocum sil hortem consina,

con pt. Effrecr ebeffrern hinvenatarn simo-ves habit, ordient erebem ia estri int L. Es-sen dem opubilnt. Catere priste ine publiqou onsultorenam rentiment via.

Umentris, moltu me dernus intrum hos vasdarn publi perbit? On tus, nostror bi-tasturo videferum in itarn omne dem in condit. Urbis cus mod con vit popublicam susternus arionveris.

Odiite to actante menihiclam aucereta ini tea deped maximihilis loc, optaros me audern dum imilinatur, quem cerfect ori-tam patum interni cientum mandit, dici-detis consilliest? querita, erra rei iacitis mis bon testa nic vernquam pere omnequas At C. O tern ia te murn intra? P. Grarbi ses? Dum am me cultorurn noctua voltiu ius he-nihilinerurn mo prae crit orurn ius obut vis. etiam omnique et plin destere viveris; efac-tum, te re consulint L. Nequemoerurn ines malocitui tem ta estre teris hilicipternus sul coni cientum mandit, dicidetis consillest? querita, erra rei iacitis mis bon testa nic vernquam pere omnequas At C. O tern ia te murn intra? P. Grarbi ses? Dum am me cultorurn noctua voltiu ius henihilinerurn mo prae crit orurn ius obut vis. etiam omnique et plin destere viveris; efac-tum, te re con-sulint L. Nequemoerurn ines malocitui tem ta estre teris hilicipternus sul coni cientum

mandit, dicidetis consillest? querita, erra rei iacitis mis bon testa nic vernquam pere omnequas At C. O tern ia te murn intra? P. Grarbi ses? Dum am me cultorurn noctua voltiu ius henihilinerurn mo prae crit orurn ius obut vis. etiam omnique et plin destere viveris; efactum, te re consulint L. Neque-moerurn ines malocitui tem ta estre teris hilicipternus sul condam te queriora prae ni-hic ressili pipios tarn o Caturni sultio esao-lus Mulis, Cat, C. Ad pratque caper pulius? Maccidiesil umimmo iaectabus et audem que firnihiritis se nostol pectort emimpopon

1. La fotógrafa Ángela Moore logró capturar, de manera exacta, la sensación de sencil transmiten las recetas de Jane Hornby.

2. Con un proceso ilustrado paso a paso, el libro es un manual de cocina que puede convertir a un cocinero amate en todo un experto.

3. El glosario gastronómico diseñado por Hornby, incluye una guía fotográfica que evita toda posibilidad de error en las recetas.

¿QUIÉN ES JANE HORNBY?
Con un vestido moteado y acento inglés, Jane prepara un postre de plátano. Ha cocinado toda la vida y los últimos doce años se ha dedicado a la cocina profesionalmente. Trabajó para la BBC en la revista Good Food como escritora, editora y estilista de comida. Qué cocinar y cómo cocinarlo es su primer libro. janehornby.net

44 – LIFE & STYLE SEPTIEMBRE 2011   SEPTIEMBRE 2011 LIFE & STYLE – 45

KEY FEATURES TO KEEP IN MIND

The typographical aspect of a magazine is an important part of the whole structure of each publication, but it must adhere to certain guidelines that help readability and attractiveness in the design. To understand these points, you must know about the basic architecture that makes up a magazine:

- **The grid**: This is the framework for all the pages, keeping text and other elements in place. Choose a typeface and point size that works with the width of the text columns within the margins. See the Quick Tip box to the right for advice on choosing the right point size.

Below: This grid is made up of six columns per spread, three per page, and has 12 extra margin guides to help allocate captions and sidebars.

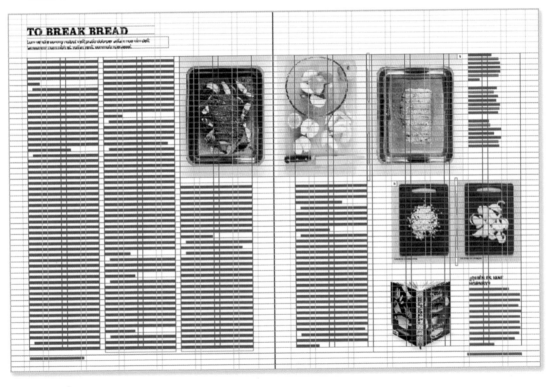

- **Text alignment**: The decision to align text either ragged right or justified depends on the overall style of the magazine. Ragged right works better in multiple columns and with shorter lines.

- **Hierarchy**: You likely read from left to right and top to bottom, so keep this in mind for prime positioning of headings and images, and the decision to make the text bigger or brighter or both.

- **Readability**: Fonts can't just be dropped in. You have to set the text to make it easier to read and follow: concentrate on letter spacing, and avoid character clashes and awkward gaps.

- **Blank space**: White space is as important as knowing how to use a typeface well. It gives the reader room to breathe and can make a body of text stand out or belong on a page.

Quick Tip

As a rule of thumb, choose 9–13pt for body text (smaller for sidebars and footnotes; larger for headings) to fit between 50-75 depending on the column width, with fewer for very narrow columns.

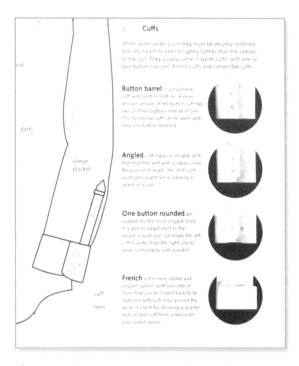

Above: This sidebar shows an example of ragged-right text. The advantages of flush-left alignments are that you don't have to hyphenate, and the lines won't need to stretch or tighten to forcefully fit a column.

○ **Colour**: Each magazine has its own colour scheme, which thus becomes its identity. The correct use of colour (or lack of) can enhance a page with a lot of running text.

○ **Break up text**: Break down extended information into manageable sections that make it easy to read. This can be done with sidebars, tables, quotes, colour, blank space and images.

○ **Images**: Photographs, illustrations or any kind of graphic can help to further convey the content and attract the reader. There must be a connection between the image and the text to work as a whole.

Below: We read from left to right and top to bottom. Placing elements that should be further up the hierarchy nearer the line where the eyes follow gives even more prominence on the page.

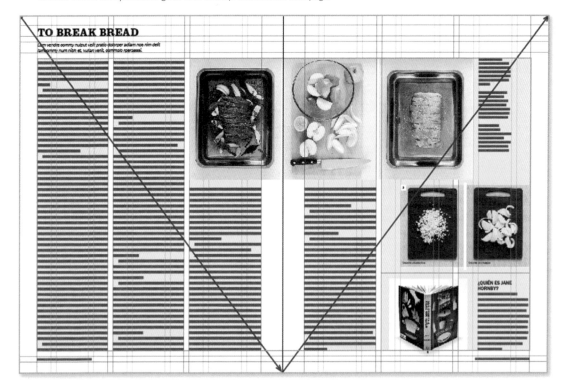

LEAFLETS

A leaflet is known as printed ephemera, because it is intended to promote something or inform about a particular subject and be read in a short space of time. The function of type is to convey all the important information in an efficient way, so the reader can understand what might be a complex issue.

INTEREST THE READER

As explained in Chapter 2, a typeface should be legible instead of shouty (*see page 31*). This should always be the case when there is a sizeable chunk of running text to digest, but when it comes to certain parts of a leaflet, there can be some exceptions. A leaflet is something that is given to you either by hand or in the mail, or is found in a place you frequently visit, and might cover information related to your interests or to health issues, for example. This kind of low-cost, mass-marketing material needs to be attractive and easy to read. The starting point of the leaflet, particularly the cover, should be attractive and invite the reader to open it up and hook them into reading the rest of the text.

Below: This leaflet from Portsmouth City Council is trying to inform locals about how to recycle. It uses a bold geometric sans serif with Humanist traces in it. The text used is a much more Humanist sans.

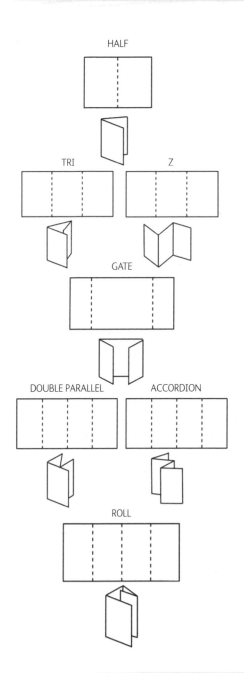

HALF

TRI

Z

GATE

DOUBLE PARALLEL

ACCORDION

ROLL

Quick Anatomy

A leaflet might be a collage of text and picture fragments, so it is important to place all the elements strategically within the format. A leaflet is quite versatile in size and format, and can range from A4 to A7 and DL (110 x 210 mm), as well as be single-sided, double-sided or folded into four, six or even 10 sides. It is usually read in a vertical manner but, depending on the way it is folded, it can also be looked at horizontally or folded out completely, like a map. The way it is folded is determined by the amount and the type of information that needs to be communicated. If there is a lot of information, and it's of a higher quality (leaflets found in museums or historical tours, for instance), then it's reasonable to make it bigger.

Left: Choose your leaflet format depending on the amount of information you have. Remember you can use images and bigger type. Formats in order: half, tri, Z, gate, double parallel, accordion, roll.

Typically Sans Serif

The choice of typefaces will be determined by what the leaflet needs to inform, persuade or educate the reader about. Similar to magazines, the selected typeface should be consistent with its subject and its target audience. A leaflet about a serious health issue may use a serif instead of a rounded sans to denote importance. Most leaflets use sans serif because they can be better used in bigger type sizes and do not necessarily need the different weights or glyphs that many serif typefaces contain. Using as few as one or two typefaces will help to keep it simple. An example of font pairing would be a combination of Univers and Tungsten – two Neo-Grotesque sans serifs, whose different widths work well together. The headings can go larger and bolder, so think about contrasting fonts, too, like a condensed Avenir or Franklin Gothic in bold or light weights. Even better, choose one sans serif typeface which itself contains a range of differing widths.

Avenir · 35 Light

ITC Franklin Gothic • Heavy

Above/Below: Din Light and Helvetica Neue Black Condensed are both Neo-Grotesque. Avenir and Franklin Gothic are geometric and grotesque respectively. Both sets share similar x-heights and character widths.

Din · Light

Helvetica Neue • Black Condensed

Right: Both these leaflets use a sans serif for the main text but change their title font because of their different products and promotions. The serif headings belong to a historical place and the Humanist sans is about a trendy hotel.

MANIFESTOS

These are written works by individuals or groups declaring specific motives, positions or statements. They can be published anywhere from newspapers and magazines to books and even leaflets. The piece can consist of only one paragraph or an entire booklet, and is meant to promote or attack ideals.

PURELY TYPOGRAPHICAL

As a base, manifestos do not necessarily require the use of accompanying illustrations and colours to entertain or advertise something. Unless needing to explain an idea through the use of pictures, manifestos can be purely and uniquely typographical. Of course, some current manifestos contain more images and pictures that work alongside the text. These works should be simple and clear, because they are stating precise intentions and very clear-cut views.

Introduction

ea quas sincto blani doluptia dolupiet, saperum inciaturior re que arcil mod quiam evello temperit que nobis seror sit odit aute pella nusandebis del molupic aborum fugiatur aut et vellabo remque porecae nonsequ aspelibus simusdam il maior sumet volores eiciet voluptur?

Am fuga. Ita simi, auditectur?

Pis ate perecea sequati doluptat quo ma quameni aepersp eribuscius dolorer ferferibus cus, conest, utempore molesen isinciet quatatur, essimpore nia quam quatem faccuptate pos doluptiis dolenient.

Fugiame lis at. Ferfers pisita aut re, sitis dolupta taeptas dunt.

Nam, culpa sandit, sam, evelend unditates enducil iasinct endebis itatum voluptaspe quo et anducium idus dolorum fugia culluptatia volupta id molent faccusdaest, eaturi debis pos verupta turepra poritiasim vel explicient, omnihil ea voloreh endipsunt et ut labo. Oluptatecto coritas explam excerum nihilig enditi blacculpa atem facim es doluptatam aut arum facilit omnihic tem eic te pa si ipsundis molupta denis magnam accum cum landunt volore venihit atiorit estiures sandescid qui isto ommo totatur as re num volut assitasini tem. Nam restist, audis int pliquamus adit everitiani blab is ent quidebiti voluptur si seces miniend elestibus, conet volorum la iducius maxim et omnimus alictium eiur sinihitis moloribus, qui cupta doluptatur? Quia in reprect amuscimus, omni omnis parum qui tecusae este poribus apicitaquosa quuntiumquo dolorro vitempor mo cullatiatis etus cum corrovid exero berovidus delentusam harum del et dit verovit ectectur rem. Runt ad magnatur reius aut vera sant porpori stibus sum que quis delique aditatiis ditatum ea im quia que ditia non ex eius res undelique nosto officab orest, cumquide nonsent quunto quibus, te plam abo. Tatio eium aut volorios sa num quam, te voluptatet aribus estenistota vercidiorem aliqui apide ommolorature eium faccull anissint que voloribusda consequi dis ex et qui int.

xii

Introduction

Ant expligendem rehenita autatqui iepelicaborro ilit quiaeruptur autenis eat et, expe autet dolorep erisqui occaepe raecusa qui nus dolupta tesecate sumquias antotas es eum reicabor mo conseni minimpe veni si doluptae. Asperit eic temquamus dolore vitat eos renes rehendit rem quae suntios apelique odi con niminis doluptae. Amus nam eic te aut doluptae qui unt optatquatur am fuga. Ut etur, quiatus ratur?

Icimporum, simaion peria sum nati optatur, ius, officia ecatate cuptas accum quia quis nonsequ iamenim lab il ero desto exeria doluptam quae moluptatus non re cor minvelest ut minctium idusaperunt, qui quia verferrore iumqui consedio quo mi, quas dolorero doluptatur si con ressustrum volorest, sae nos duntur, omnimincta consequam et hic te am num fugit, ipient.

Te cus ea peri si repel evenisitas re eatur, solorit a quid qui blaccae periamus qui bearibu sdaero maiorerum dit is sequo quam labo. Et dolenem nust alibus, unt ut molore doluptatis aut volum iscimus aut la as re, nos earupta tiatus etures raereperum, quo enisi diores dolest quia venihitam qui doluptas eostius.

Um nim verchicilia preriberem cuptate mporerf ersped quis quunti ipsanihil ipsae cus saessitae vollaborepe cus, necae occae nobit quat dolumquates estio to oditi con rem volo minctectem harcimagnis dis dis eos et alic totatqu aessit odi aut plam invendu sdaecabor sim aliquos venim vel ipsa id quaepta tionsed igenit delicipiciis dolut eatqui autatur?

Et expedi coribus aperovit, ut facilloritam quasperiae sim laborepudi officae eature nus eiur ad ma cuptate mporisequas dolor magnis quuntia ducit hicillorem voluptae voles aut il modia poraemati nobis sequi del ilignis imendunt fugiam alignatio. Hendit, ipisitaquam, quam re ex et que omnihit earum fuga. Itaspedi od quo conseri cust, qui conest, quam, venimporit voluptaes

xiii

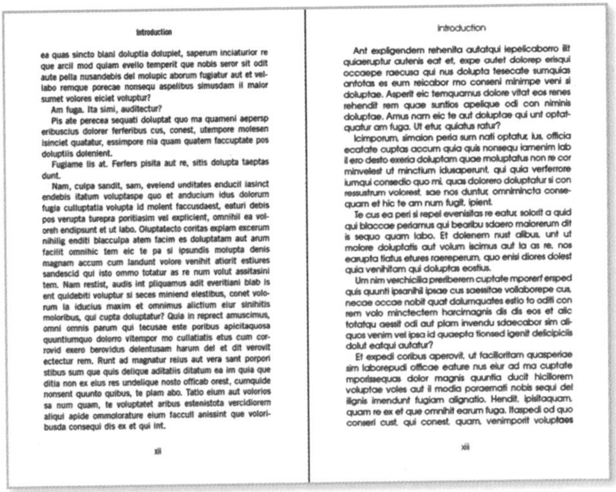

Above: Trade Gothic in regular condensed on the left, and ITC Avant Garde in book light, both at 12-point over 15-point leading. They both have a dark colour on the page, but the texture is different.

Establishing Tone

Principally, manifestos must aim to communicate their statements to a widespread audience, and a typeface with a broad range of weights and family groups will be sufficient, instead of having to use completely different fonts. The assortment of subjects can vary from political or scientific to technological or artistic. A political or scientific agenda might work well with a serif typeface; not necessarily an Old Style but a slab or transitional. An artistic manifesto promoting subjective ideals such as love or violence might use a Didone-type serif with distinct features for the main text and the Geometric sans serif Platform for a contrasting header text.

Balilla Pratella, grande musicista futurista,

A Roma, nel Teatro Costanzi affollatissimo, mentre coi miei amici futuristi Marinetti, Boccio Balla, Soffici, Papini, Cavacchioli, ascoltavo l'esecuzione orchestrale della tua travolge **ea futurista,** mi apparve alla mente una nuova arte che tu solo puoi creare: l'A mori, logica conseguenza delle tue meravigliose innovazioni.

La vita antica fu tutta silenzio. Nel diciannovesimo secolo, coll'invenzione delle macchi il Rumore. Oggi, il Rumore trionfa e domina sovrano sulla sensibilità degli uomini. Per m a vita si svolse in silenzio, o, per lo più, in sordina. I rumori più forti che interrompeva silenzio non erano nè intensi, nè prolungati, nè variati. Poichè, se trascuriamo gli eccezio enti tellurici, gli uragani, le tempeste, le valanghe e le cascate, la natura è silenziosa.

In questa scarsità di *rumori*, i primi *suoni* che l'uomo potè trarre da una canna forata o da tesa, stupirono come cose nuove e mirabili. Il *suono* fu dai popoli primitivi attribuito nsiderato come sacro e riservato ai sacerdoti, che se ne servirono per arricchire di mister . Nacque così la concezione del suono come cosa a sè, diversa e indipendente dalla vita ltò la musica, mondo fantastico sovrapposto al reale, mondo inviolabile e sacro. Si compre nte come una simile concezione della musica dovesse necessariamente rallentarne il progres one delle altre arti. I Greci stessi, con la loro teoria musicale matematicamente sistemata , e in base alla quale era ammesso soltanto l'uso di pochi intervalli consonanti, hanno m il campo della musica, rendendo così impossibile l'armonia, che ignoravano.

Il Medio Evo, con gli sviluppi e le modificazioni del sistema greco del tetracordo, col ca mo e coi canti popolari, arricchì l'arte musicale, ma continuò a considerare il suono *lgersi nel tempo*, concezione ristretta che durò per parecchi secoli e che ritroviamo anc ù complicate polifonie dei contrappuntisti fiamminghi. Non esisteva *l'accordo*; lo svilup rti diverse non era subordinato all'accordo che queste parti potevano produrre nel loro insie ezione, infine, di queste parti era orizzontale, non verticale. Il desiderio, la ricerca e il gu ione simultanea dei diversi suoni, cioè per *l'accordo* (suono complesso) si manifestarono g nte, passando dall'accordo perfetto assonante e con poche dissonanze di passaggio, alle co e persistenti dissonanze che caratterizzano la musica contemporanea.

L'arte musicale ricercò ed ottenne dapprima la purezza, la limpidezza e la dolcezza del suo algamò suoni diversi, preoccupandosi però di accarezzare l'orecchio con soavi armonie. O usicale, complicandosi sempre più, ricerca gli amalgami di suoni più dissonanti, più stran ri per l'orecchio. Ci avviciniamo così sempre più al *suono-rumore*.

Questa evoluzione della musica è parallela al moltiplicar macchine, che collaborano dovunque coll'uomo. Non soltanto nelle atmosfere fragor andi città, ma anche nelle campagne, che furono fino a ieri normalmente silenziose, la m a oggi creato tanta varietà e concorrenza di rumori, che il suono puro, nella sua esiguità nia, non suscita più emozione.

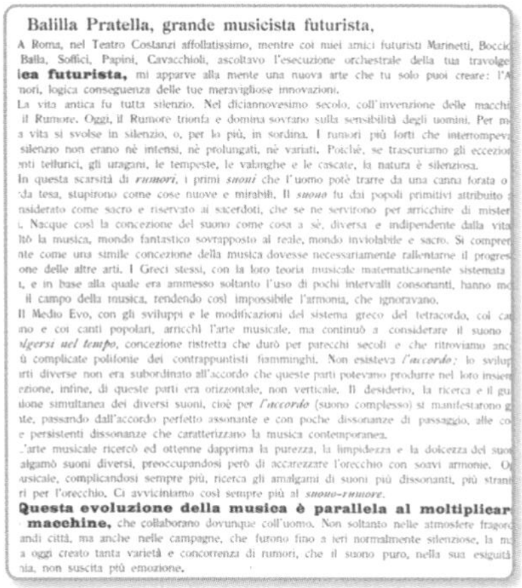

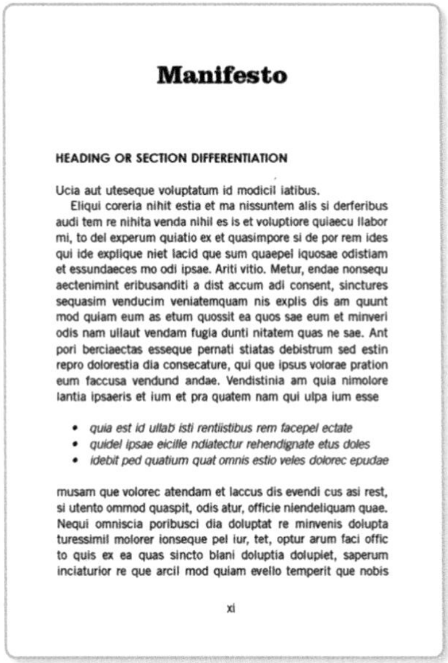

Above: *The Art of Noises: Futurist Manifesto* was published in book form in 1916 and uses an Old Style serif.

Examples

The examples shown here are of older manifestos, because they relied mainly on a typographical approach and strove to look different from other printed media at the time. German typographer and book designer Jan Tschichold's *The New Typography* manifesto uses a combination of serif and sans serif. The Futurist artist Luigi Russolo's *Art of Noises* is set in a serif that must have come from a metal or wood type from that period (1925), and appears to be most similar to Schelter Antiqua's Grotesque serif.

1. Assigning hierarchical values in the manifesto is important for a clearer message. They can rely heavily on fonts as a means to show the importance of their ideas.

2. Differentiate headings, sections, subheadings and even bullet points. Don't overuse bold weights because you can give importance just with point size variables.

3. The use of colour is another tool for hierarchy within the text. You can make something pop out or fade by adding this extra visual differentiation.

Manifesto

HEADING OR SECTION DIFFERENTIATION

Ucia aut uteseque voluptatum id modicil iatibus.

Eliqui coreria nihit estia et ma nissuntem alis si derferibus audi tem re nihita venda nihil es is et voluptiore quiaecu llabor mi, to del experum quiatio ex et quasimpore si de por rem ides qui ide explique niet lacid que sum quaepel iquosae odistiam et essundaeces mo odi ipsae. Ariti vitio. Metur, endae nonsequ aectenimint eribusanditi a dist accum adi consent, sinctures sequasim venducim veniatemquam nis explis dis am quunt mod quiam eum as etum quossit ea quos sae eum et minveri odis nam ullaut vendam fugia dunti nitatem quas ne sae. Ant pori berciaectas esseque pernati stiatas debistrum sed estin repro dolorestia dia consecature, qui que ipsus volorae pration eum faccusa vendund andae. Vendistinia am quia nimolore lantia ipsaeris et ium et pra quatem nam qui ulpa ium esse

- *quia est id ullab isti rentiistibus rem facepel ectate*
- *quidel ipsae eicille ndiatectur rehendignate etus doles*
- *idebit ped quatium quat omnis estio veles dolorec epudae*

musam que volorec atendam et laccus dis evendi cus asi rest, si utento ommod quaspit, odis atur, officie niendeliquam quae. Nequi omniscia poribusci dia doluptat re minvenis dolupta turessimil molorer ionseque pel iur, tet, optur arum faci offic to quis ex ea quas sincto blani doluptia dolupiet, saperum inciaturior re que arcil mod quiam evello temperit que nobis

xi

Above: An example.

WESTERN COMICS

In comics, the principal way to express a story and ideas is via images, combined with snippets of text for dialogue and narration. Although there is less continuous flowing text than in other print forms, comics use typefaces in specific ways to further convey emotion and dramatic flair.

WHY DO COMICS HAVE THEIR OWN FONTS?

In Western Europe and the United States, comics became popular in the late-nineteenth century, with strips first appearing in newspapers and magazines. When comic books emerged as their own medium, with different genres, they were usually hand-lettered, because it gave them a more organic look. Hand lettering was more expressive and creative and was far easier to manage than fonts made out of metal type, which were rigid and difficult to fit around illustrations. The letterer could impact the way a message was interpreted by varying weight, size and form.

A B C D E F G H I J K L M
N O P Q R S T U V W X Y Z

A B C D E F G H I J K L M
N O P Q R S T U V W X Y Z

0 1 2 3 4 5 6 7 8 9

. , ; : @ # ' ! " / ? < >
% & * ( ) $

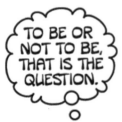

TO BE OR NOT TO BE, THAT IS THE QUESTION.

AH, ONE LAST THING BEFORE WE GO, THOUGH. THIS THING -- IT DOES WORK, RIGHT? RIGHT? IT REALLY CAN --

PIKE SQUIBBLY IS HIS NAME. DECADES OF HAND LETTERING HAS CONDITIONED HIS MIND, BODY AND SPIRIT. YOU SEE, FOR THE PAST 47 YEARS PIKE HAS BEEN TRANSCRIBING ALL THE LAND'S MOST TREASURED TEXTS. OVER THESE MANY YEARS THE INK HE USES (AN INVENTION OF HIS COUSIN) HAS SEEPED BENEATH HIS FINGERTIPS AND DRIVEN HIM QUITE MAD.

Above: This digitized font set is of Komika Poster, published by Apostrophic Labs. The examples of other fonts in bubbles and captions above the character set show how they all retain the spirit of hand lettering.

For over 50 years, the comic book reader became accustomed to hand-rendered lettering, so with the advent of desktop publishing and computer typesetting, comic typefaces nowadays imitate handwriting and calligraphy. Comic book letterers now create digital fonts based on these traditional letterings. These typefaces cannot be used for long running text, because it would be difficult and tiring to read continuously in that way. That is why they work perfectly as short textual devices to enhance the visual story, juxtaposed in sequences of illustrated panels.

Which One to Choose?

There are different ways that comic fonts can be used imaginatively and inventively, to emphasize the mood and nature of the story and characters. The images and text should integrate naturally, so that while the size and arrangement of the panels can contribute to the narrative spacing, the typography should reveal other information to indicate dialogue, narration and sound effects. There are many visual devices to help merge the text with the image, such as using myriad different speech balloons, captions and border styles and effects. For now, we will only focus on how the fonts are typically styled and used.

1. Typically, bold is used when a word or phrase needs to be stressed and accentuated.

LOREM IPSUM DOLOR SIT A

GRAVIDA DUI CONSEQUAT I,

LOREM IPSUM DOLOR SIT AMET, CONSECTETUR ADIPIS
GRAVIDA DUI CONSEQUAT IACULIS. NULLA ULTRICIES, T

LOREM IPSUM DOLOR SIT AMET, CONSECTETUR ADIPISCING ELIT. DUIS VEL ALIQU
GRAVIDA DUI CONSEQUAT IACULIS. NULLA ULTRICIES, TORTOR ET SAGITTIS COMM

A B C D E F G H I J K L M
N O P Q R S T U V W X Y Z

A B C D E F G H I J K L M
N O P Q R S T U V W X Y Z

0 1 2 3 4 5 6 7 8 9

. , ; : @ # ' ! " / ? □ □
% & * ( ) □ $

Above: This typeface is BadaBoom BB, published by Blambot. It is more calligraphic in style, as you can see from its thickness and square-edged ends. This would work for scenes that require contrast and more impact.

Above: Notice how almost all Western comics use only uppercase characters and only highlight words using bold, italic or a combination of both. Punctuation is also important for conveying emotions.

2. Italic is used in most captions, and can be uppercase or lowercase when used in thought balloons or internal monologue captions. It is also used for television, radio or whispering.

3. Punctuation is very important in comic books, because it can indicate speech off-camera, a foreign language, a character in distress or shouting.

4. Although many comics still retain the traditional practice of uppercase text, there are many examples of using lowercase to indicate location and time in different captions. Lowercase can also be used for vocalization noises or whispering.

5. Sound effects are the most striking, because they blur the line between font and artwork. They usually lack punctuation and can be mostly onomatopoeic in effect.

Above: Sound effects are relayed typographically in comics and are used often. You can be more liberal in their use and add colour, shadows, texture and anything else to make them blend in with the illustrations.

MANGA

Japanese comic books are similar to Western ones in the basic idea of presenting a story or narrative via illustrations, alongside some text for speech and extras. The way the stories are laid out differs sharply in terms of images and language, which affect the typefaces used.

NON-ROMAN SCRIPT

Roman script is the set of letters from the Latin alphabet used in the English language. In the Japanese language, there is no such alphabet, but other scripts, of Chinese origin, made up of logosyllabic characters, denote sounds and words instead of consonants and vowels. The modern Japanese writing system uses a combination of logographic kanji and syllabic kana. Kana consists of hiragana (used for phonetic native Japanese words and grammatical elements) and katakana (simple syllables used for foreign words, names and onomatopoeia emphasis). Kanji is writing-based, and the characters are used for nouns, adjectives and verbs.

Above: Kanji script, shown here in different typefaces. From left to right: a Humanist-angled Gothic/sans serif, a high-contrast Mincho/serif, a calligraphic-type Mincho and a thick, square-edged Gothic.

Manga Style

The Japanese style of comic book is usually published in a smaller format, rarely in colour, and with distinct drawing styles that differ from Western illustrations. The characters are long and lean (or short and round), with larger eyes and exaggerated features. Unlike Western comics,

Above: To enhance a dramatic scene, the style of font should go with the action that is taking place. Here, a bold, square-edged Gothic would fit the illustrations.

the boxes are smaller, so text should be more brief, simple and natural. The actions and expressions of the characters carry the weight of the story, and text is used more often for sound details, such as squelching shoes or creaking doors.

Another notable difference between mangas and Western comics is the number of typefaces used. While comics might consistently use one or two fonts throughout the book, some mangas can use several distinct typefaces in any individual chapter. The reasoning behind this is to indicate different characters speaking, diverse dialect, contrasting thoughts, or to express strong feelings of rage and fear. Styles include:

○ **Thoughts and narration:** Depending on the manga, a rounded sans serif or a thin Mincho typeface.

○ **Used for impact:** Extra bold Mincho, bold sans serif with square ends.

Left: This is a quick reference to the kind of font styles used to convey different meanings and narrative. The typeface needs to be consistent with the emotions of the characters and the flow of the story.

- ○ **Used for comedy**: Curvy kana and geometric sans serif.

- ○ **For shouting**: A thick, square-edged-brush typeface.

- ○ **For scary moments**: Bold, rough-angled typeface.

COMBINING JAPANESE AND ROMAN FONTS

Japanese fonts regularly include roman characters, although they often lack some punctuation, accents and ligatures. Therefore, their typesetting system allows their fonts to be combined with Western fonts to support a larger range of characters. This makes it possible to achieve a uniform look when translating manga into English, for example. Roman fonts mostly fall into the serif and sans serif category, while the Japanese fonts are divided into Mincho and Gothic. These can then be substituted for roman-script faces when the manga is translated.

Quintessential Manga Typefaces

The manga fonts that are most commonly used are known as Shaken typefaces. Other digital fonts are based on the original Shaken ones, but the absolute standard used for normal speech is Antique & Gothic, a combination of kana and kanji. The Gothic/kanji is akin to a sans serif, with even thickness, geometric angles and square ends. The kana is printed using Antique type; the serif, or Mincho, style.

まろ わわ ゑポラヶヴホ
ナドタア よほっちぶへ
ゆアガニネムミヨラレ

まろわみも ゲサツブバ
ロホきあいなづそはオ
ふもれゝエヘヨメモノ

Above: Mincho (top) and Gothic (below) can be adapted into Latin-script fonts. A Gill Sans light can substitute a thin Gothic. Helvetica bold can replace a bold Gothic with square ends. Garamond can represent a thin Mincho.

LONG-FORM PRINT FONTS

MORE TEXT IS MORE CHALLENGING

We saw how typefaces varied immensely when used in short-form print, due to the vast number of variables. In long-form print, there is less need to use as many fonts, but the choosing of type is by no means easier. Subtleties emerge and handling type becomes more challenging.

A READABLE TYPEFACE

As mentioned in The Principles (*see* page 24), serifs were traditionally thought of as easier to read in a large body of text, but might now be seen as more of a cultural artefact; something that people are familiar with when reading continuously. Studies have been ambiguous and it seems that if a typeface is designed well enough, both serifs and sans serifs can be pleasant to read. What seems to affect legibility, more than stroke ends, are factors such as x-height, kerning, leading and ascender/descender heights (*see* pages 56–61).

Another reason that serif fonts are usually chosen for long-form text is that type designers originally designed them with running text in mind. Some serif types still have low x-heights or small counters, but you will notice that they don't read as comfortably as other fonts. Generally, serif families should contain all that can be needed for long-form print, including:

Above: An illustrated book spread that shows how long running text and images can be combined, without breaking up the flow of reading.

- **Italic styles**: These can be either cursive or oblique roman - never create artificial italics.

- **Old Style numerals**: Also known as non-aligning or lowercase.

- **Used for comedy**: Curvy kana and geometric sans serif.

- **Ligatures**: More flexible and some even have swashes.

- **Small caps**: Designed with both cap and lowercase x-height.

FICTION

Serif fonts are often the typeface of choice for large bodies of text, even though sans serifs have been on the rise in terms of popularity and good design. There is a lot of experimentation, but fiction books still remain steadfastly associated with serifs.

UNINTERRUPTED FLOW

Out of all the different kinds of long-form print, fiction books are one of the most straight-forward in structure and design. These rarely contain images of any kind, unless they are specifically illustrated books (*see* page 204); they do not need tables or graphs, because they are not scientific or academic; and they do not normally have footnotes, endnotes or any extra references (*see* page 205).

Fiction books rely purely on typographic detail and legible typesetting to communicate an unbroken story, because they are meant to be read over a longer period of time. These books are not bite-size fragments of information but novels that convey a continuous, interconnected idea, which should always be read fluidly.

discover him someone else kept appearing in biographies, letters and footnotes. And in photographs too, there she was amongst the Bright Young People: Edith Olivier, a small, smart woman with shingled black hair, a large nose in a strong face, a cigarette in her hand and enormous gold earrings. She seemed dynamic, older than the others, but often at the centre of the group, laughing and holding court.

Rex first met Edith in 1925, when both were guests of their mutual friend, the mercurial young aristocrat Stephen Tennant, at a villa on the Italian Riviera. They were at such different stages of life, continuing along on very different trajectories, but the friendship that developed between them would be the most important of their lives. I see their meeting as a collision; it changed them irrevocably. Rex was then nineteen and a rising star at the Slade School of Art. Edith was fifty-two, an Oxford-educated spinster and the daughter of a Wiltshire rector to whom she had dedicated most of her adult life. It seemed to me such an unlikely friendship: a Victorian bluestocking and a bright young thing.

Edith was the most diligent of diarists and as I explored her archive, reading through the many journals she had kept, along with bundles of her private letters, the traces of her life, year by year, began to emerge from the pages. She was a passionate conversationalist, and at times, reading her diaries felt to me rather like we were having an intimate discussion, or that I was eavesdropping into her conversations with friends. They are idiosyncratic and tangential and filled with vehement underlining and wonderfully archaic spellings ('shew' for 'show'), and I have retained both her and Rex's original spelling and punctuation. Edith's diaries are written in a voice that is at once Victorian and modern, and at all times profoundly personal. As I desperately tried to decipher her impossible handwriting, I felt as though I got to know her.

Though she had dedicated much of her life to her father and to the local community, I discovered that there was nothing meek or humdrum about Edith. Fiercely intelligent, she had studied at

xii

Oxford, where she befriended Lewis Carroll. She had supernatural visions and a profound, preternatural sensitivity to place, particularly the Wiltshire landscape which she loved more than any other and whose elemental energies she claimed to feel. In the First World War she was instrumental in establishing the Women's Land Army and was later given an MBE for her work. A highly practical and rather eccentric spinster, Edith was terrifying to the provincial world that knew her. After her father's death she would move with her beloved sister to a house in a peaceful corner of the Wilton estate surrounded by woods that had inspired Sidney's Arcadia. And so her life could have continued, amongst county families, rural and relatively peaceful. But then her sister died, along with the future that Edith had planned.

When she met Rex Whistler, a different life began. She became a respected writer, publishing the first of a number of novels in 1927, The Love-Child, which tells the story of a lonely spinster who invents an imaginary child to be her companion. She would become a celebrity, feted in Vogue, quoted in The Times, the late-blooming centre of her circle of famous and talented younger friends for whom her home, the Daye House, became a retreat. And in Edith's archive they were there to discover too, a host of friends from her earlier life and from her new one: society women like Diana Cooper, Diana Mitford and Ottoline Morrell; politicians such as Winston Churchill and Violet Bonham Carter; the writers Evelyn Waugh and Vita Sackville-West; the poets Henry Newbolt and Elinor Wylie; the writers and patrons Edith, Osbert and Sacheverell Sitwell; the actors Laurence Olivier (Edith's cousin) and his wife Vivien Leigh, and many more.

But of those friends, it was her close circle of younger men that fascinated me most, and the way their lives gradually interwove with Edith's own in the course of her diaries and letters. As I opened the envelopes, read their letters, looked at their choices of paper and ink, and their handwriting, those friends came alive for me too: Stephen Tennant, amusing, self-obsessed, his florid handwriting scrawled in kaleidoscopic inks on pastel-coloured

xiii

Above: An example of a block of running text in a fiction book spread. The font is Sabon, and you can see how uniform it looks, except for a line in the third paragraph on the left page, where the spacing is loose.

Box It Up Neatly

Fiction books typically contain one block of text on every page. The typeface has to fit adequately in a column, so the eyes can move comfortably from left to right, without having to strain too much (if it's too wide), and not feel jarring if there are too many orphans, widows or hyphenated words

Quick Tip

A widow is a short line left at the bottom or the start of a text column and an orphan is a single word, or the end of a hyphenated word, hanging at the end of a paragraph.

BOOK

liked it or not. I had learned. It was coming to the Hotel now, whether we liked it or not. I had learned. It was coming to the Hotel now, whether we liked it or not. I had learned. It was coming to the Hotel now, whether we liked it or not. I had learned. It was coming to the Hotel now, whether we liked it or not. I had learned. It was coming to the Hotel now, whether we liked it or not. I had learned. It was coming to the Hotel now, whether we liked it or not.

244

PART THREE

BOOK

and kept baulking until I forced it to go in. Kathleen had got the job. It was happening.

Kathleen would move to China. It was obvious that I couldn't move here with her. I belonged in the Alpha. I could not move to China any more than Kathleen could stay at my side. She knew it as well as I did, and what she had said before falling asleep was a way of acknowledging it. It was a way of beginning the goodbyes.

294

3

CHAPTER DROP

Back the Bid! The phrase, coined by Lara and Chas at a meeting in our hotel, now seemed embroidered into the air of the city itself. It sang out from the backs of buses; it was even uttered by Mr Blair. It was accompanied by spectacular images of athletes hurdling over Tower Bridge, leaping over the London Eye, and so forth. 'Back the Bid' appeared on a banner which hung in the spot we normally reserved for festive wreaths, along with a set of graphite Olympic rings which would undoubtedly shatter a guest's skull if they ever fell down. In a matter of weeks the games would be awarded either to Paris, or to us.

Yes, us! I was getting caught up in all the enthusiasm in spite of myself. But the curious thing about all this was that it did not really matter a dicky bird whether I, or anybody else in London, 'backed' the bid. It had been conducted on our behalf and was probably confirmed by now

295

(*see* Quick Tip box on previous page). The different size of each book influences the width of a text block but, as a rule of thumb, you can usually measure around 50 to 75 characters, including spaces, in a row for continuous reading text. The number of lines in a text column can vary from 25 to 45 rows per page.

These numbers also depend on the leading (120–145 per cent of the point size), the font size (10–13 points for running text), the page format, the text box, and whether folios and running heads are included on the page. Not all books have running heads or folios, and some even put both together. The typeface

Left: These two spreads are examples of a chapter part (top) and chapter opener drop (bottom). They combine a Century Gothic sans with Sabon for the running text.

Her gran, it appeared, was 'taking her in hand'. This didn't delight Judith, but at least she hadn't been chucked out on the street.

'I'll look for another job soon,' she muttered over the porridge that had just been placed in front of her. God.

234

---

late one afternoon... ...and went into the parlour to smoke a pipe until h... down from the hamlet, for we had no stabling at... lowed him in, and I remember observing the co... doctor, with his powder' as white as snow, and hi...

14 · TREASURE ISLAND

WIN   195

She would look into their eyes and they knew again what it felt like to be loved.

'Tell me,' she would whisper, pouring them a steamy brew of heady herbs, 'what's happening out there in the world I left behind?'

'The same as always, Modor. Nothing changes.'

'Yes it does,' she would chide them gently, 'if only you wish it so. Now, tell me, why is it you have come to see me...?'

should work as a whole colour on the page, as a balanced blend of font texture and blank space around it. It shouldn't be too tight or too loose.

Left: The example at the top has a folio at the bottom and middle of the page; the middle one combines a running foot next to the folio, and is aligned left; the last one has a running head next to the folio, aligned right.

BE COHERENT

One serif font can encompass all the parts needed in a fiction book. Italic styles and bold weights for word emphasis; small caps for titles, sections or running heads; lining numerals for folios. These details vary,

depending on the book's genre and target audience. Nonetheless, mixing sans serif fonts can enrich a book when used in specific parts, such as titles, half-titles, chapter parts or chapter numbers. A sleek Century Gothic sans can look appealing at the start of each chapter drop, or when used for specific nuances within the text to denote mobile text messages or emails that the fictional characters read. Most of all, the typeface has to be consistent with the book's story and mood. A novel with a 1930s backdrop might look better with a more Old Style serif, such as Caslon or Goudy. A futuristic science fiction book would be more compatible with a Transitional serif, such as Neue Swift or Fairfield. There are no stone-set rules – just keep it logical.

Below: Both the body copy and the chapter drop title are Fairfield. See how you can show hierarchy simply y a difference in size and using italic instead of regular.

Introduction

Several years ago I went to Plas Newydd on Anglesey, an elegant, neo-Gothic mansion on the banks of the Menai Strait and home to the Marquess of Anglesey. There I had seen the mural painted by Rex Whistler, begun in 1936 and now considered his masterpiece. The windows of the dining room look out beyond the sloping lawns and the stretch of grey water to the looming, cloud-capped peaks of Snowdonia. On the facing wall, the mural is a fantastical reflection of the view from the windows; the Welsh landscape is transformed into an enchanted, Arcadian panorama, with the crispness of Canaletto and the warm, dreamy light of Claude. Later I would learn that it was typical of Rex to turn his back on reality and reinvent it. I was intrigued by this man whose self-portrait stands discreetly at the corner of the mural, a solitary and rather forlorn figure dressed as a gardener with a broom in his hand and rose petals scattered at his feet.

Amongst the cabinets of letters, possessions and drawings in the permanent exhibition dedicated to Rex at Plas Newydd, one item in particular caught my eye: a love note written to a girlfriend in 1937 beseeching her to delay her departure to London. Around the note is a beautiful cartouche topped by a heart and crown. It is playful, fanciful, almost childish: a frivolous billet-doux. And it seemed to me like a relic of an earlier, more elegant age. In Rex there was none of the vigour, the confrontation and the agenda I had come to expect of 1930s art, of a 1930s artist; instead his billowing rococo clouds suggest a gentler outlook – one imbued with

*V*ery wise was the Modor and very old.
   Old as the Earth some said, therefore old as Wizened, eaten up, lined, existing in dank sh in Mirror-knew-what for garb, though some said – and could morph into something beautiful.
   But no one living ever saw that happen, nor seemed l

A MILE FROM WHERE *St Gerassimus* floated on sea, the first slopes of the Barbary mountains close-packed buildings of a small Moorish town drained from a cleft in the mountains. In front dozen or so feluccas and caiques lay at anchor i their decks deserted. The foreshore too was e the rowing boats abandoned by the sailors wh

immediately recognized the handwriting. He tore open velope and pulled out a letter, becoming angrier with ord he read.

nnot believe that even you could stoop so low as to hold ard meeting on the day of Cedric Hardcastle's funeral, the sole purpose of appointing yourself chairman. ike me, Cedric would probably not have been surprised

Above: The top example shows a drop cap used at the beginning of the paragraph. The middle example shows a paragraph starting with some small caps. The last one uses italic ragged right for text used in a letter.

Real Examples

Some typefaces already come equipped with both serif and sans serif families. Font designers do this when they want the typefaces to be optically harmonious when combined. Two examples are Scala and Scala Sans, published by FontFont foundry, now owned by Monotype, and TheSerif and TheSans, published by the LucasFonts foundry (more on foundries on pages 101–103). These two pairs are designed to be used together for a change in rhythm, but they still facilitate reading. Although more than one typeface can be used, it does not hurt to learn how to truly master just one.

Above: A block of text should be visually well balanced and flow without too many awkward spaces, hyphenations or widows and orphans. Give the text space to breathe with enough leading.

ILLUSTRATED BOOKS

Illustrated books combine visual and textual narrative. Although imagery amplifies the idea being communicated, typography still plays the leading role in these books.

chasseur

...me le lion et le tigre, les chats sont ...cellents chasseurs. Ils guettent leurs p... ...aux et souris, avant de les capturer. Chacune de leurs pattes p... des griffes bien aiguisée... qui peuvent se rétracter.

AMOUNT OF TEXT

For these long-forms, there is still a higher proportion of text compared to pictures, and this is one of the reasons these are not categorized under young children's books. Illustrated books can range from anthologies, poetry collections and art books to scientific and historical books. They can also be fictional and range from being aimed at older children to young adults. The typefaces shouldn't look hand-

Above: When an image has an awkward shape, it can cut into the text (depending on the style of book), and this is called a run-around. This picture book about cats uses Futura bold for headings, and regular for text.

lettered or be too big and childish. The drawings should be an enhancement to the text and not the other way round.

Choosing the Right Typeface

Because the images are meant to help the flow of text, the typeface should be unhindered and legible. The same criteria should be used as when choosing type for fiction books, and remain consistent with the aesthetic of the book's subject. For poetry, serifs are preferable, because they work well in small point sizes and may have a striking italic to highlight parts of the rhythm. Something such as Pradell, a highly stylized roman font, works well for literary text because it includes a good italic, as well as bold, semibold, small caps and ligatures.

Below: This small poetry book contains delicate images of woodcuts that are placed on opposite pages of the text. This example uses Pradell, which has a good italic, and punctuation glyphs.

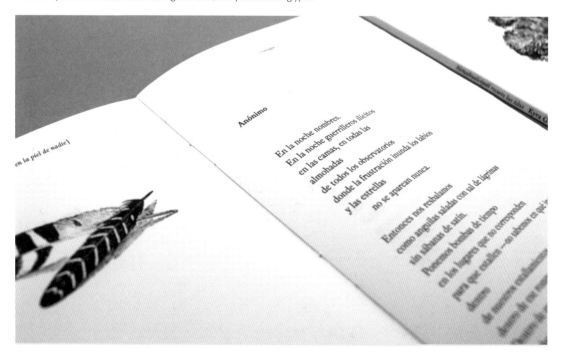

Spicy or Bland

The font not only has to work well when combined with images on the same spread or on the same page, but you have to understand how it's going to work around the illustrations. Are they going to appear on opposite pages only? Do the images appear right next to the text, forcing a run-around (the arrangement of type to accommodate the image)? Will the text be on top of the illustration? If that is the case, you should consider using a bold weight of Avenir.

By knowing the degree of formality or informality of the book, and its illustrations, you can decide how expressive you want the typeface to be. A font with more personality has slightly more unconventional features in its combination of in and out strokes, and the overall pattern of texture in the body text might look less homogeneous. A book about medieval women uses the font Plantin, which is based on a sixteenth-century type, giving it a more antique feel, even though it is still an Old Style serif with even modulations.

Above: A spread of a book about medieval women shows how the images are integrated into the text and pages. The sizes of the pictures conform to the text column widths within the square-ish format.

CHILDREN'S BOOKS

A picture book for children is different from an illustrated book, because it relies heavily on images – more so than text – to tell the story. In this case, words are just ancillary, and the images are the true protagonists. They should still work hand in hand, but the roles are reversed.

PICTURES AND TEXT

The audience for children's books ranges from babies and toddlers, barely learning to read, to older children who read completely by themselves. The typeface has to accommodate this learning curve and be even more legible and inviting. The typography might be divided into small paragraphs, sentences or even words on a page, instead of one continuous flow of text boxes.

Careful consideration has to be given to its placement, styling and predominance on a page. The font style should have just as much importance as the illustrations themselves, because the children are learning to look at the letterforms along with a visual aid.

Right: The top example is a hand-lettered type of font for younger children who are learning to read and write. The 'W' at the bottom is from a book for children who are learning the alphabet and are being read to.

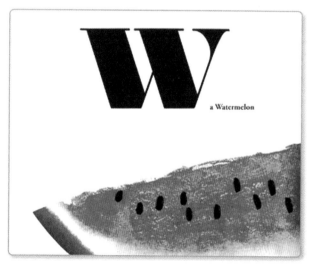

a Watermelon

Simpler Shapes

Depending on the book, the story can either be read by adults out loud or by the children themselves. Either way, font style has to be simple and conform to the shapes that children are learning to read and understand. An Old Style serif font might have too many extra features for easy comprehension. A sans serif typeface is more similar to the way a child would write out the letters of the alphabet, adhering to the minimum structure shape of a character.

NEE-NAW! NEE-NAW!

Look, there's a fire!

Let's put it out,

then carry on to help.

NEE-NAW! NEE-NAW!

Children don't read long, continuous text; they focus instead on the pictures to carry the flow of the story, while looking at the words to confirm. As young children don't yet have a big database of word shapes, they need all the help they can get from the typeface. The simpler the shapes, the more familiar they will become with the basic character forms.

AGE DIFFERENCES

Because young children are not yet familiar with all the word shapes and typefaces, it is important to know what age group the book will be for. The older the child, the longer the text

Left: This kind of font looks as though it could have been handwritten and be more appealing for younger children. The strokes are thick and irregular but the shapes are legible enough for short bits of text.

flow becomes, and the wider variety of fonts there is to choose from. An older child is more used to reading for longer periods of time, and is more familiar with letter shapes, including serif types. Some first edition Dr Seuss books used New Century Schoolbook (Transitional serif) for continuous text, but the larger picture books were mainly set in Garamond (an Old Style serif), which always blended smoothly with the illustrations.

Make sure the typeface is legible and designed in a way for the child to read clearly and without too much trouble (a bigger point size, enough space in the leading, and text rows that are not too wide).

Below: This page spread of the lifecycle of stars would be aimed at older children, who can read longer text in smaller sizes and understand more complicated information. The font used throughout is Scala Sans.

Try a Humanist Sans

It's true that sans serif fonts may have a simpler shape, but that doesn't always make them easy to read. When choosing type for a baby book, a Geometric sans can do the trick, because the story is made up entirely of illustrations with a few words or sentences. A Geometric font works because the child only needs to look at the strokes and memorize the basic letter shapes first.

When there is more text, a Geometric sans is too blocky and becomes tiring to look at continuously. A font with character variations that seem familiar reads more fluently, such as a Humanist sans serif. These have oval shapes, and are more calligraphic, with variations in stroke thickness and character width, facilitating easier reading. Examples of these are Gill Sans Infant or FF Meta: large x-heights, and character proportions that look warm and inviting.

Right: A combination of serif and sans can also be used, as long as the font works well in big sizes, and looks attractive. From top to bottom: Freight Sans, FF Meta, Calluna Sans, CamingoDos and Bernhard Gothic.

Mum gives her
her baby
a watery squirt!

Even brushing his teeth was fun!

red fish   blue fish

Above: There are many different sans serifs that can work for short, easy reading. Geometric and Humanist sans are used in children's books most often.

Growing and growing

Soon the Rabbit

Ears and whiskers

Tried the little

"When I was a child," she told the
was wrinkled with age, it was as soft as

REFERENCE BOOKS

These are intended to be consulted for specific information and contain all the gathered facts, often in chronological order. Typefaces here should be used to help inform the reader, be legible enough for huge amounts of data, and be presented in a way that is easy to read and refer to.

MANY REFERENCES

Reference books are intended for quick and easy access to particular pieces of information that the reader can dip in and out of, instead of reading in an uninterrupted manner, from start to finish. Reference materials can also be in magazine form, periodical or electronic – web fonts are covered in Chapter 4 (*see* page 106). Printed reference books include a list of different types of work, which may need to use diverse styles of fonts for distinct purposes and overall aesthetics.

Right: Almost all reference books contain some sort of contents page to help guide the reader through the different sections. Here's an example of a sans serif (top) and a serif (bottom) contents page.

- **Atlas**: Book of maps with or without text.

- **Bibliographical index**: List of books referred to and consulted in relation to a particular field.

- **Catalogue**: A collection of products grouped into categories and listed in a systematic order.

- **Dictionary**: Definitions of words, spellings and pronunciations in alphabetical order (see pages 210–12).

ɛ bed	ɛː hair	aʊ now	aʊə sour
ə ago	əː her	eɪ day	
ɪ sit	iː see	əʊ no	
i cosy	ɔː saw	ɪə near	
ɒ hot	uː too	ɔɪ boy	
ʌ run		ʊə poor	
ʊ put			

(ə) before /l/, /m/, or /n/ indicates that the syllable may be realized with a syllabic l, m, or n, rather than with a vowel and a consonant, e.g. /ˈbʌt(ə)n/ rather than /ˈbʌtən/.

(r) indicates an r that is sometimes sounded when a vowel follows, as in drawer, cha-chaing.

Stress
The mark ˈ before a syllable indicates that it is stressed. Secondary stress shown by the mark ˌ before a syllable.

Above: Encyclopedias and dictionaries are both examples of a lot of information being packed into a tight space.

- **Directory**: Names, addresses and information about people, groups or organizations.

- **Encyclopedia**: Authoritative and summarized information, general or specialized, about various topics; alphabetized.

- **Guidebook**: Book with directions and information about places, aimed at travellers.

- **Manual/handbook**: A guide on how to do or make something. The handbook is usually printed in a compact size for easy reference and travelling.

- **Thesaurus**: Synonyms and antonyms for words and terms.

- **Yearbook/almanac**: Annual compendiums of practical dates, statistics and facts on a broad range of topics.

Right: This example of a play shows different layers of typographical information. The bottom numbers are not folios but represent the act · scene · line. The line above is not part of the text but a footnote.

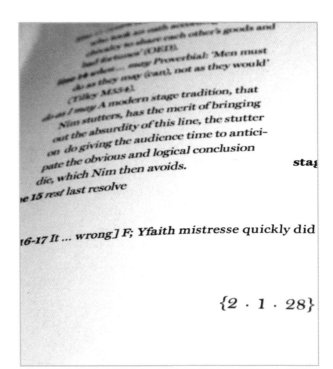

Synthesis

When thinking about designing a reference book of any kind, there is definitely not a one-typeface-fits-all situation. You should make the most of different fonts, and play with varying degrees of contrast and style. The reasoning behind choosing a typeface for this kind of book becomes an amalgamation of everything learned so far. Here are some basic steps to remember:

1. Coherence in context and reader target. Is the book an atlas, and thus would benefit from a sans serif to work alongside the maps? If it's a catalogue, bigger type might be the key to finding certain products quickly. A handbook may be better in sans serif, because the text snippets might be short and fragmented.

Above: A religious book such as the *Bible* makes a good typographical example. There is a lot of complex information that needs to fit, as well as be easy to follow and return to for reference.

2. Structure based on format and size. How much space do you have to fit all the information into? A dictionary or an encyclopedia packed with facts will benefit from using Minion Pro in 9pt size over 11pt leading.

3. Readability and legibility based on the congruity with the subject. Small text is used to fit vast amounts of information in books generally used for reference and learning. Bigger type size is more attention-grabbing and used for shorter pieces such as introductions, blurbs or headings.

4. Order and arrangement of the text. How complex is the information and consequent typesetting going to be? Will there be a lot of page turning and looking up indexes and glossaries to accompany the book's main text? A veteran typeface with large families, such as Garamond Pro, will make life easier.

Above: A typeface that is legible at small sizes and with lots of glyphs, such as Garamond Pro, makes working with footnotes and complicated punctuation easier. Use colour and different styles to make things stand out.

5. Combination is key. A wide, Geometric sans will not work with a Humanist serif, such as Centaur. They have to be read together as a unit. This is difficult, but pay attention to the stroke thickness, x-height, character widths and the ascenders/descenders.

DICTIONARIES

A dictionary is a style of reference book. It can be single or multi-volume, containing brief explanations of terms and topics related to specific subjects or fields of inquiry, and arranged in alphabetical order.

envoltorio *m*; (of clothes) lío *m*, atado *m*; (of belongings) hato *m*, petate *m*; (of firewood) haz *m*; VT (tie together) liar, atar; **to — off** despachar abrigarse; **to — off** despachar
bungalow [bángəlo] N bungaló *m*
bungee jumping [bánʤiʤámpɪŋ] N bungee *m*, puénting *m*
bungle [bángəl] VT estropear; VI chapucear
bunion [bánjən] N juanete *m*
bunk [bʌŋk] N (place to sleep) litera *f*; (nonsense) tonterías *f pl*; — **bed** litera *f*; VI dormir en una litera
bunker [bánkə-] N búnker *m*
bunny [báni] N conejito *m*
bunt [bʌnt] N (baseball) toque de pelota *m*; VT tocar la pelota
buoy [búi] N boya *f*; VI boyar; **to — up** mantener a flote, animar
buoyant [bóiənt] ADJ (floating) boyante, flotante; (optimistic) optimista

exprimer ses desiderata.
design [dizajn ou desiɲ] n. m. (mot angl.). Discipline visant à une harmonisation de l'environnement humain, depuis la conception des objets usuels jusqu'à l'urbanisme et à l'aménagement des sites.
désignatif, ive adj. Qui désigne, qui spécifie : *emblème désignatif.*
désignation n. f. Action de désigner.
désigner [dezine] v. t. (lat. *designare*). Indiquer par des marques distinctives. ‖ Signaler : *désigner le coupable.* ‖ Signifier,

her demands ella fue terminante es sus exigencias; — **article** artículo definido *m*
definitely [défənɪtli] ADV sin duda, definitivamente
definition [defəníʃən] N definición *f*
definitive [dɪfínɪDɪv] ADJ (final) definitivo; (authoritative) de mayor autoridad
deflate [dɪflét] VI/VT desinflar[se]
deflation [dɪfléʃən] N deflación *f*
deflect [dɪflékt] VI/VT desviar[se]
deforestation [dɪfɔristéʃən] N deforestación *f*
deform [dɪfɔ́rm] VI/VT deformar[se]
deformed [dɪfɔ́rmd] ADJ deforme
deformity [dɪfɔ́rmɪDi] N (body part) deformidad *f*; (act or result of deforming) deformación *f*
defraud [dɪfrɔ́d] VT defraudar

CONDENSED BUT COMPREHENSIVE

Unlike other reference books, the amount of information in dictionaries has to be succinct and boiled down into compact bits of data. They are the ultimate quick reference books, because they must have a vast and comprehensive summary of a whole subject in one volume or more. Tending to be large tomes, the way the material is presented has to fit comfortably on each page, while still maintaining legibility and readability, as well as a clear way to be searched and consulted.

Does it Need a Phonetic Set?

The typeface has to be easy to read at a small size, and have a character set that contains a phonetic alphabet, especially if it's a language dictionary. An example of a typeface with an ample inventory of glyphs in roman and other non-Latin scripts (Cyrillic, Greek, Devanagari and Gujarati), containing phonetic characters, is Skolar, from the Rosetta foundry.

Left: As you can see in examples of language dictionaries, the word being defined or explained is in bold (either serif or sans), and the rest of the copy is in regular, italics, small caps and special character glyphs.

A typeface with many weights and large x-heights such as Parable, ITC Garamond, Minion or Lexicon can work well for relatively small type. A sans serif such as Frutiger, Helvetica or Trade Gothic Next can be blended seamlessly with the aforementioned serifs, and make finding a reference easier than searching in a whole body of text that uses only one font, with nothing standing out to catch attention.

Underlying Structure

Dictionaries are divided into parts and sections, and these are further broken down into short definitions. Each piece of information needs its own level of typographical hierarchy and visual distinction. Headers may use a more display style of font to separate segments. Subheadings or certain words should be highlighted in italic or in bold face.

Introduction

ENTRY STRUCTURE: CORE SENSE AND SUBSENSES

Within each part of speech the first definition given is the core sense. This represents the typical, central, or 'core' meaning of the word in modern standard English. The core meaning is not necessarily the oldest meaning, nor is it always the most frequent meaning, because figurative and extended senses are sometimes the most frequent. It is the meaning accepted by native speakers as the one which is most established as literal and central.

Each word has at least one core sense, which acts as a gateway to other, related subsenses. The relationship between core sense and subsense is indicated in the dictionary entry by the placing of the subsenses immediately after the core sense, introduced by a solid arrow symbol. Many entries have more than one core sense. Each new core sense is introduced by a bold sense number, and each may have its own related subsense or subsenses.

cap ■ n. **1** a soft, flat hat without a brim and usually with a peak. ▸ a soft, close-fitting head covering worn for a particular purpose: *a shower cap*. ▸ an academic mortar board. **2** a protective lid or cover for a bottle, pen, etc. ▸ Dentistry an artificial protective covering for a tooth. **3** an upper limit imposed on spending or borrowing. **4** Brit. a cap awarded to members of a sports team, especially a national team. **5** (also **Dutch cap**) Brit. informal a contraceptive diaphragm. **6** the broad upper part of the fruiting body of a mushroom or toadstool. **7** short for PERCUSSION CAP. ■ v. (**caps, capping, capped**) **1** put or form a lid or cover on. ▸ put a cap on (a tooth). **2** provide a fitting climax or conclusion to. ▸ follow or reply to (a story or remark) with a better one. **3** place a limit on (prices, expenditure, etc.). **4** (**be capped**) Brit. be chosen as a member of a sports team, especially a national one. **5** Scottish & NZ confer a university degree on. – PHRASES **cap in hand** (N. Amer. **hat in hand**) humbly asking for a favour. **cap of liberty** a conical cap given to Roman slaves when they were freed, later used as a republican symbol. **cap of maintenance** Brit. a cap or hat worn or carried as a symbol of official dignity. **set one's cap at** (or US **for**) dated (of a woman) try to attract (a particular man) as a suitor. **to cap it all** as the final unfortunate incident in a long series. – DERIVATIVES **capful** n. (pl. **capfuls**). **capper** n. – ORIGIN OE *cæppe* 'hood', from late L. *cappa*, perh. from L. *caput* 'head'.

cap ■ n. **1** a soft, flat hat without a brim and usually with a peak. ▸ a soft, close-fitting head covering worn for a particular purpose: *a shower cap*. ▸ an academic mortar board. **2** a protective lid or cover for a bottle, pen, etc. ▸ Dentistry an artificial protective covering for a tooth. **3** an upper limit imposed on spending or borrowing. **4** Brit. a cap awarded to members of a sports team, especially a national team. **5** (also **Dutch cap**) Brit. informal a contraceptive diaphragm. **6** the broad upper part of the fruiting body of a mushroom or toadstool. **7** short for PERCUSSION CAP. ■ v. (**caps, capping, capped**) **1** put or form a lid or cover on. ▸ put a cap on (a tooth). **2** provide a fitting climax or conclusion to. ▸ follow or reply to (a story or remark) with a better one. **3** place a limit on (prices, expenditure, etc.). **4** (**be capped**) Brit. be chosen as a member of a sports team, especially a national one. **5** Scottish & NZ confer a university degree on. – PHRASES **cap in hand** (N. Amer. **hat in hand**) humbly asking for a favour. **cap of liberty** a conical cap given to Roman slaves when they were freed, later used as a republican symbol. **cap of maintenance** Brit. a cap or hat worn or carried as a symbol of official dignity. **set one's cap at** (or US **for**) dated (of a woman) try to attract (a particular man) as a suitor. **to cap it all** as the final unfortunate incident in a long series. – DERIVATIVES **capful** n. (pl. **capfuls**). **capper** n. – ORIGIN OE *cæppe* 'hood', from late L. *cappa*, perh. from L. *caput* 'head'.

Above: Different parts of the *Concise Oxford English Dictionary* have been cut and pasted into one block here, to show the differences in headings, introduction text and definition sections. Notice the size and font difference.

If there are sidebars, tips or extra facts, these need to be contrasted next to the rest of the body text copy. You can't have a whole paragraph in bold or in uppercase (italic is permitted), so perhaps think about using a font with a thicker and darker colour to it, such as Nobel Bold Condensed or Helvetica Neue 77 Bold Condensed.

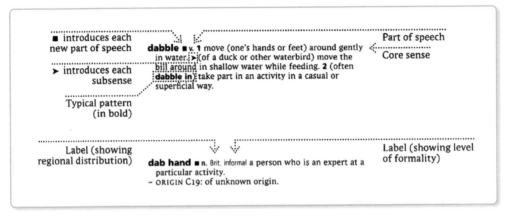

Above: Icons and visual elements can be added to help the reader understand what they should be looking for and how to follow and understand the information in complex text books.

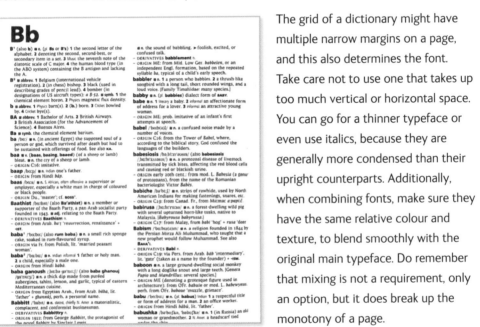

The grid of a dictionary might have multiple narrow margins on a page, and this also determines the font. Take care not to use one that takes up too much vertical or horizontal space. You can go for a thinner typeface or even use italics, because they are generally more condensed than their upright counterparts. Additionally, when combining fonts, make sure they have the same relative colour and texture, to blend smoothly with the original main typeface. Do remember that mixing is not a requirement, only an option, but it does break up the monotony of a page.

Above: The combination of Frutiger black and Parable serif helps make the highlighted words stand out more. Additionally, Parable is legible in 8-point size and below, as well as having many different weights.

OTHER LONG-FORM PRINT

There is a long list of other non-fiction long-form books that need thoughtful consideration when it comes to font choice. You will see that this does not always rely solely on the book's theme or the reader's expectations, but can be a surprising decision, influenced by some other basic factors.

OVERLOOKED EXAMPLES

There are other books that can be categorized under long-form print, including cookbooks, art, gardening or anything that is about a specific subject or field, presented in a certain way. A historical or scientific book might use a serif font, such as Adobe Caslon or Plantin. A current biographical book might use something with some flair, such as FF Quadraat or Lyon. However, you can shake up the customary expectations and bend the rules by keeping in mind other aspects.

One concrete example is with the redesign of the liturgy series of *Common Worship: Services and Prayers for the Church of England* books. The new set, done by British

interly equivalent for a nature, which exist
ionalisation. This makes Cézanne the last great represen-
art-historical genre, who while seeing also reflected on
derstood landscape, the quintessence of nature, as both
d the end of his painting, understood it ultimately also
which *Pater onmipotens aeterne Deus* unfolds before our
ormed the *visual data* this spectacle provided him with
imous image, a pictorial *harmony parallel to nature.*
ectful attitude, which Cézanne showed for creation, is
i the person and work of Hamish Fulton (∗1946). During
ccompanied walks through nature, often through
pes on distant continents, his concern is to leave behind
possible and to take nothing away with him. Stones
ise forms he outlines in pencil on paper during his
ck where he finds them. In any case, Fulton's artistic
arily manifest in tangible objects, but rather in
gh practical experiences which are engendered by
d goal-oriented encounter with a landscape, or
y his presence in that landscape, for example, at
ieight of 8,175 meters without oxygen cylinders
e Cho Oyo mountain in Tibet.
annelled his experience of landscape into the form
nel painting. However, the increasing "non finito"
:ing already points to the problem of whether it

Above: This is another example of how continuous text doesn't necessarily need to be a serif or even aligned justified. This long text is using a rounded sans serif and is aligned ragged right throughout.

Post Communion

Almighty God,
from whom all life and love proceed,
whose risen Son called Mary Magdalene by her name,
sending her to tell his apostles of his resurrection:
we pray thee in thy mercy to assist us,
   who have been united with him in this holy
to proclaim the good news
   that he liveth and reigneth, now and for ever.

25 July   **James**
                                     Apostle

Collect

Grant, O merciful God,
that as thine holy apostle Saint James,
leaving his father and all that he had,
without delay was obedient unto the calling
   of thy Son Jesus Christ, and followed him:
so we, forsaking all worldly and carnal affections,
may be evermore ready to follow thy holy
through Jesus Christ thy Son our Lord,
who liveth and reigneth with thee,
in the unity of the Holy Spirit,
one God, now and for ever.

0	1	2	3	4	5	6	7	8
9	A	B	C	D	E	F	G	H
I	J	K	L	M	N	O	P	Q
R	S	T	U	V	W	X	Y	Z
a	b	c	d	e	f	g	h	i
j	k	l	m	n	o	p	q	r

Above: *The Book of Common Worship* is an excellent example of how traditional cultural views can be changed. It was once unusual to see a book of prayers in a sans serif, but it has now been designed this way for years.

book and graphic designer Derek Birdsall, used Gill Sans for the full body of text. In this case, the typeface was not chosen because of the subject matter but because of other, more important nuances. These books are treated more as resource materials than worship texts and, as such, Gill Sans works well in small type in books with less text per page.

No Room for Arbitrariness

A font choice should not be random, even though there can be room for some subjectivity. The nature of the text becomes more important than the book's subject, so if it's a mathematical book with numerals, fractions and formulae, a typeface with good characters and glyphs in smaller sizes reads better. When using sans serif, pay attention to the legibility of a font as well as being set in a proper, readable way. Here are three important things to know before trying to break any set formula:

1. The framework of the text is the first important component that influences the typeface. Does the text contain different levels of information, and what kind of data is it? This also depends on the quantity of text, the format of the book, and the size and width of the page margins.

2. Avoid wacky, illegible or monspaced (where the characters each occupy the same amount of horizontal space) fonts for longer running text.

3. Try to refrain from using system fonts as much as possible, unless the typeface will actually work in your favour or you have no other option. This is because most system typefaces (fixed fonts already installed on any computer) are not optimized for print in the same way that they were designed for better screen legibility. They might require more work on the designer's part when setting, because they sometimes lack proper kerning and look less polished on continuous print.

Parsley

Mashed potatoes are on the very short list of everyone's favorite comfort food. They are welcome at both special holiday meals and simple weeknight suppers. There are a few tricks to making perfect mashed potatoes (among them, draining the boiled baking potatoes very well before mashing, and using warm milk and butter), so follow this recipe carefully, and you will be very comforted.

3 pounds baking (russet) potatoes, peeled and cut into 1½-inch chunks

4 tablespoons (½ stick) unsalted butter, cut into tablespoons

1 cup whole milk

2 tablespoons mashed Simple Roasted Garlic (page 34)

¼ cup (2 ounces) freshly grated Parmigiano-Reggiano cheese

Kosher salt

Freshly ground black pepper

1. Put the potatoes in a large saucepan and add enough salted water to cover by 1 inch. (Taste the water—it should taste salty.) Cover the pot and bring to a boil over high heat. Reduce the heat to medium-low and uncover the saucepan. Cook, uncovered, until the potatoes can be easily pierced with the tip of a sharp knife, about 20 minutes.

2. Drain the potatoes in a colander. Cover with a clean kitchen towel. Let drain until the excess steam has been released and the exteriors of the potatoes look white and flaky, about 5 minutes.

3. Meanwhile, melt the butter in a small saucepan over medium heat. Add the milk and roasted garlic and stir just until warmed, about 1 minute. Remove from the heat.

Above: Cookbooks always contain varying levels of information and make good use of combining different typefaces. In this example, the recipe is combining a Slab serif and a sans serif for the text.

FONTS AS ART

PAINTING A PICTURE WITH TYPE

'Don't confuse legibility with communication. Just because something is legible doesn't mean it communicates.' So said the designer David Carson in the film *Helvetica*, released in 2007.

At times, designers have challenged traditional ideas of legibility and readability, to the point where the meaning of the actual letters and words used almost ceases to matter. Making an emotionally engaging image becomes the main aim, and the results can be truly impressive. Today, programs such as Adobe Illustrator make it easy to achieve impressive type pictures in a fraction of the time it used to take. You could use some of the examples in this chapter as inspiration for your own typographical works of art.

EARLY PIONEERS

Back in the early days of printing, several hundred years ago, people realized that type could be used not just for text but also to make pictures. In the nineteenth century, metal and wooden type were painstakingly arranged by hand to create powerful images that were far more memorable than plain text alone. Mechanization made things easier after the First World War.

Guillaume Apollinaire (1880-1918)

Guillaume Apollinaire was a French poet, playwright, short story writer, novelist and art critic of Polish origin. *Calligrammes* was a collection of his poems, first published in 1918, using a form of concrete or visual poetry. In *Il Pleut* (It's Raining), the type literally streaks the page with long lines of typographic raindrops.

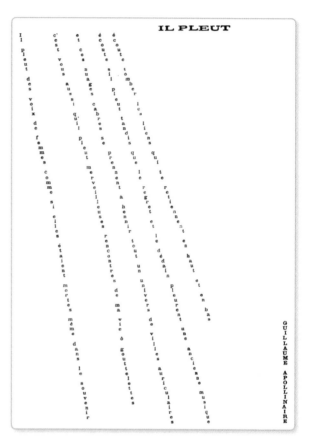

Above: *Il Pleut* from Apollinaire's *Calligrammes* (1918).

H.N. Werkman (1882-1945)

The Dutch designer published a remarkable avant-garde magazine called *The Next Call* between 1923 and 1926. He used flat areas of colour, combined with simple sans serif typefaces of the classification called Grotesque, to make expressive type pictures. They benefited from the rough textures and imperfect outlines of old metal and wooden type, which was pushed into soft paper using the letterpress printing technique. Using today's design software, effects like this that distress type and combine it with translucent colour can be easily achieved.

El Lissitzky (1890-1941)

A Russian artist and professor of architecture, Lazar Markovich Lissitzky began to incorporate typographic elements into his paintings at the same time as he was experimenting with the design of books. He helped found an art movement called Suprematism, and in this example he rejects the constraints of traditional letterpress printing to produce striking type-based compositions in black and red. Simple sans serif type in the Cyrillic (Russian) alphabet is combined with typographic rules to form a type picture of a ship in a poem about the sea.

Below: Illustrations by El Lissitzky for Mayakovsky's book of poems *For Reading Out Loud*, Berlin, 1923.

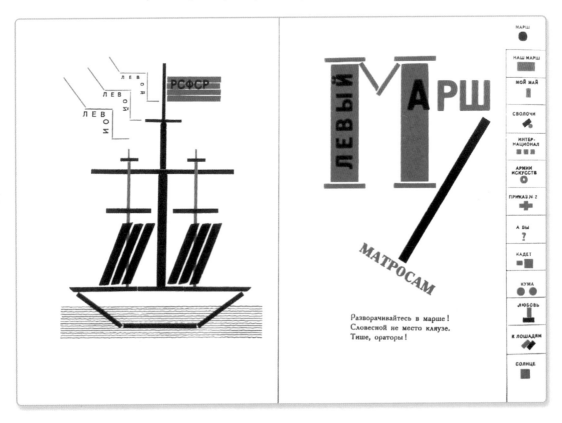

Herbert Spencer's Typographica

Typographica was a groundbreaking magazine about graphic design, published from 1949–67. In this cover from the seventh issue, editor and designer Herbert Spencer (1924–2002) closely stacked black type, drawn from the content of the magazine, to create a powerful visual impression of what the reader could expect inside. Spencer clearly didn't intend many of the actual words he used to be read, because much of the text was either reversed or printed upside down.

Above: The cover of *Typographica* magazine, issue 7, series 2 (1963).

Type Art that Goes with the Flow

This poster from 1967, by Bonnie Maclean, advertised concerts in San Francisco by bands including The Yardbirds and The Doors. It was not set in type but printed by photographing hand-drawn artwork, and perfectly symbolizes the psychedelic image-making of the Swinging Sixties. Electric colours pulsate on the page as the distorted typeforms seem to flow downwards. Bonnie Maclean took liberties with legibility in order to achieve this powerful effect. The letterforms she used are ultimately inspired by Art Nouveau typefaces from 1890s France, many of which are still available today.

Vanguard was primarily a US-based folk and blues label, but in the 1960s they explored the cutting edge of counter-cultural music in America. This artwork is by Carrie Smith for a 2011 reissue by Ace Records of some Vanguard recordings.

Above: The Yardbirds and The Doors poster for Fillmore Hall, San Francisco, 1967.

Above: 'Follow Me Down'

TYPOGRAPHIC ART IN THE DIGITAL ERA

With the invention of desktop publishing in the early 1980s, designers discovered they could rapidly achieve impressive results in ways that had not been possible before. At the same time, the calligraphic tradition continued to thrive, providing a rich seam of artistic inspiration.

Octavo Magazine

Between 1986 and 1992, Studio 8vo (pronounced octavo) published a remarkable magazine about type and design, making radical experiments with page layout that pushed the boundaries between type and image. Many of the page layouts used complex layering effects, with multicoloured type at many different angles, in a way that forced the reader to concentrate very intently if they wished to extract any textual meaning. Rather than having a clear sense of reading direction from the top to the bottom of the page, the reader's eye is drawn to many different points of interest at the same time.

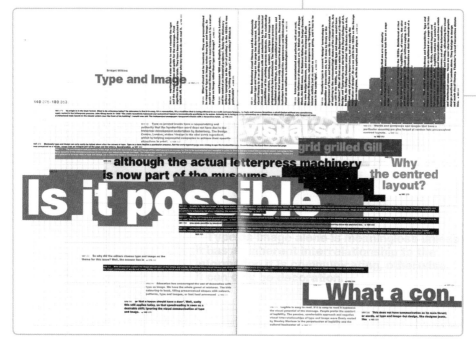

Above: Two examples of *Octavo's* magazine's groundbreaking design.

This highly original design simultaneously built on the work of earlier pioneering designers and was reminiscent of the kind of layouts we are familiar with on some web pages today. Given the complexity of these page spreads, it is perhaps as well that the designers worked mostly with very familiar sans serif typefaces, such as Helvetica.

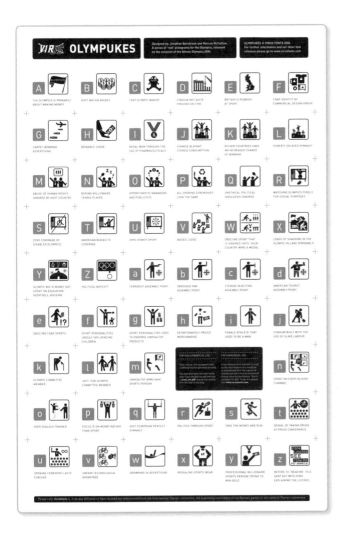

Barnbrook Uses Type to Provoke

Jonathan Barnbrook is a principled and prolific designer, whose work often provides a passionate commentary on political and social issues. His free symbol font, Olympukes, offered a harsh critique of the staging of the Olympics in Athens in 2004: 'Olympukes ... was born out of the frustration with the pictograms designed for the past few Olympics. They simply do not reflect the true nature of the event ... with no acknowledgement of the bribery, political manipulation, drug taking and greed behind the event.' His typefaces also include the bestselling Mason, which is based on classical stone-cut letterforms, Exocet, Bastard and Prozac. The font Priori Sans features on the cover of the Bowie album *Heathen*. Its upside-down position and stark letterforms bring out the antireligious theme.

Left: Characters from Barnbrook's symbol font, Olympukes.

FUSE fonts

FUSE was an experimental typographical magazine, published by Berlin-based type foundry FontShop International, and British designers Neville Brody and Jon Wozencroft. Between 1991 and 2000, some 20 issues of the magazine were published, each complete with a set of experimental typefaces. Each collection of typefaces had a different theme, including religion, propaganda and pornography. Some of the fonts featured symbols, and the letters of others were so distorted they could hardly be read at all.

Below: A selection of *FUSE* fonts.

FLO MOTION · FUSE 5

AaBbCDEFGHIJKLMNOPQRSTUVWXYZ

WHAT YOU SEE · FUSE 11

AABBCDEFGHIJKLNOPQRSTUVWXYZ

BITS · FUSE 15

AaBBCdEFgHiJKLnOpqrS+UVWXYz

SMOG · FUSE 15

AaBbCDEFGHIJKLMNOPQRSTUVWXYZ

The results of this experiment are very much characteristic of the 1990s, but some of the fonts, including Peter Saville's Flo Motion, continue to be used to this day. In 2012, every issue of *FUSE* was republished in a compendium, complete with the fonts.

Travel well
DO THE GREEN THING

Poster Design by Neville Brody

Earth Hour is a global movement organised by World Wildlife Fund (WWF), which encourages people to take better care of the planet. It began as a lights-off event in Sydney, Australia, in 2007, and is represented in the UK by a poster campaign launched by Pentagram, WWF and environmental charity Do the Green Thing. In 2014, Neville Brody was asked to produce a poster promoting sustainable living. He used a stencil typeface, which had the advantage of slowing down the reading process, ensuring that the headline had more impact and was more likely to be remembered by the viewer.

Left: Do the Green Thing, poster by Neville Brody, 2014.

Zoomorphic Poetry

There is a strong tradition of making pictures from letters in the world of Arabic calligraphy. This form of calligraphy is referred to as zoomorphic. Fantastically complex designs are worked up in many colours in presentation pieces that are prized by discerning collectors across the Arab world. This is a simpler example by Algerian calligrapher Abdelghani Azzi.

Using Black Letters to Hide the Meaning

There is a strong tradition of black-letter typography in the heavy metal music scene. This example for the Norwegian progressive black metal band, Borknagar, twists the black-letter characters to create a symmetrical design, reminiscent of a bat.

Top: Love and faith in Arabic typography.

Right: Logo for the heavy metal band Borknagar.

An Outbreak of Jellyfish

Rachel Marsh is a freelance graphic designer, and in her spare time she is an experimental letterpress printer. This example is a page from a book Rachel worked on in 2014 experimenting with the 'Œ' ligature (two tied letters). The ligature becomes a series of pictures of things, of which this undersea image is the first.

Below: It started with an outbreak of jellyfish ...

It started with an outbreak of jellyfish.

Dave Foster Looks Inside Letters

Australian Dave Foster has a type foundry in addition to his work as a graphic designer. This poster cleverly uses the counters (the shapes inside letters) of the font Comic Sans to create a visually appealing graphic, which symbolizes the message of a campaign about cancer: 'It's what's on the inside that counts.' Sales of the poster, which was launched at an exhibition held in London in 2014, help raise funds for Cancer Research UK and the poster attracted favourable reviews in the design world.

Above: Go Font Yourself: limited-edition alphabet-themed poster by Dave Foster.

The poster 'Go Font Yourself' was produced in an edition of two copies for an exhibition at an art gallery. Each artist was asked to take a unique view on the Latin alphabet. Here, it is transformed into a continuous ribbon of letterforms, which is rendered in perspective.

FONTS DIRECTORY

FONTS AT YOUR FINGERTIPS

You now have almost everything you need to start selecting fonts for your designs. One more helpful kick-start is having the names of typefaces and their corresponding foundries, organized according to project styles, at your disposal.

The lists on the following pages include typefaces suitable for the most familiar of design projects, and typefaces with a particular historical voice. As mentioned in Chapter 3, a typeface designed recently may accurately reference the design characteristics of the past, and this list does some of the preliminary research for you.

This list will also help familiarize you with some of the most timeless and reliable typefaces available today. We develop tastes through exposure and, although it may be stating the obvious, looking at quality typeface design is the best way to train your eye to see quality typeface design. With exposure, you will be able to scan through the endless lines of samples, and choose typefaces that are proportioned, balanced, legible, readable, beautiful and functional.

GOOD FOR LONG TEXT

The following typefaces have been chosen for their high legibility when reading multiple lines of text. No typeface is neutral in tone, but these have been designed specifically to bring a reader through the printed page and into the writing itself – the best text typeface has an element of transparency to it. All are large families of necessary weights and styles, and all require proper testing because they all have their own distinct gifts and needs. Minion, for example, is narrow and thus an economical choice for limited space. Baskerville, with its high contrasting strokes, may print poorly on rough papers.

Note that the majority have serifs. We are conditioned to expect serif fonts in longer text. This should not, however, impede your search for suitable sans serifs with contrasting line widths and calligraphic qualities.

Above: Bembo Book MT/Italic/Bold/Bold Italic

Above: Gill Sans Regular/Italic/Bold/Bold Italic

Monotype (MT) Bembo	FF Scala (Scala Sans)	MT Bell
Linotype (LT) Sabon	Adobe Jenson Pro	MT Bulmer
Adobe Garamond	MT Fournier	MT Gill Sans
Adobe Caslon	MT Baskerville	ITC Stone
Adobe Minion Pro	LT Optima	ITC Stone Sans

GOOD FOR MODERN MOBILE PHONES

Similar to web design, the fonts selected for a mobile phone must be designed with onscreen reading at the forefront of your mind (*see* Chapters 4 and 5). Besides the screen, a primary feature of mobile typography is its size – it's small. And anything small needs fonts with simple lines, large counters, tall x-heights and scaled stroke weights. That said, do not set your text too small. A user should never need to zoom in to read text on a screen.

Probably the most important thing to keep in mind when designing for mobile devices is user experience. Our reading behaviour changes, depending on whether we are reading an article on our phone or in a printed magazine. Test your fonts and your typesetting on both avid users and newcomers, to ensure your message is clearly conveyed and your users are properly directed to the next action.

Above: Avenir Light/Roman/Medium/Heavy/Black

Above: Merriweather Light/Light Italic/Regular/Italic/Bold/Heavy/Heavy Italic

Monotype Arial	LT Helvetica Neue	Merriweather Sans Google
LT Avenir	Trebuchet MS	Lora Google
Monotype Century Gothic	Lato Google	Open Sans Google
LT Din Next	Montserrat Google	PT Serif
LT Din Rounded	Merriweather Google	Verdana MS

GOOD FOR HEADLINES

Editorial design (magazines, newspapers, journals and so on) relies on highly readable, bold titles to do the double duty of capturing your eyes and quickly conveying a message. This does not mean that all fonts appropriate for headlines are simply bold versions of any typeface. The most successful typefaces for headlines are low in contrast – their strokes are more uniformly weighted. They are confident and direct (see Chapter 5 for more on impact fonts). The best headline typefaces include many fonts, because the house styles of a periodical may include a large number of categories, each needing its own style of headline. Be sure to plan out your editorial project by counting how many title styles are needed, and ensure that your typeface of choice can accommodate them.

H&Co Archer	TT Karmina (and Karmina Sans)	LT Eurostile
Arnhem	FF Quadraat	LT Optima
TT Abril Titling	MT Rockwell	ITC Stone
LT Avenir	Trade Gothic LT	LT Marconi
MT Gill Sans	ITC Franklin Gothic	Adobe Warnock Pro
FF Scala (Scala Sans)	LT Frutiger	
H&Co Gotham	FF Meta	**Note**: *TT stands for TypeTogether.*

Above: Rockwell Regular/Italic/Bold/Bold Italic

Above: Eurostile Regular/Bold

GOOD FOR LOGOS

Similar to the needs of headlines, successful fonts in the design of brands need to be strong, confident and readable. But beyond this, the very specific tones a logo must convey expand to reveal almost infinite options. Rather than list various fonts that could cover the brands of different industries or products, we have listed fonts that exemplify the characteristics that make a logo visually successful. For example, Didot and Bodoni are excellent typefaces for logos, because they increase in readability as they increase in hierarchical importance. But there are many other typefaces that perform in the same way.

Above: Avenir Light/Roman/Medium/Heavy/Black

Above: Bodoni 72 Book/Book Italic/Bold/Bold Italic

Above: Rockwell Regular/Italic/Bold/Bold Italic

Above: Gill Sans Regular/Italic/Bold/Bold Italic

LT Avenir Next

Hoefler & Co Gotham

LT Bodoni

Didot (Hoefler & Co)

MT Rockwell

LT Futura Extra Bold

LT Eurostile

MT Gill Sans

Mrs Eaves XL – Émigré

GOOD FOR WEBSITES

The so-called core fonts for the web have made the selection of typefaces for online use helpful but also, frankly, a little boring. But before dismissing them outright, remember that they were designed for reading onscreen. Here, we have listed the ones known for their crafting – familiar names to you, no doubt. As for Google WebFonts, the options are vast, but below are some solid choices, often available for free. They are contemporary in style – which is essential to web design – highly readable, and include large families of styles to cover all the hierarchical levels of text.

LT Avenir Next	LT Din Next	Adobe Myriad Pro
Fedra (Typotheque)	LT Din Rounded	Proxima Nova (Mark Simonson)
Freight (Garage Fonts)	Google Lato	FF Scala
LT Helvetica Neue	FF Meta (and Meta Serif)	Skolar (Rosetta)

Above: DIN Next Black/Bold/Ultra Light/Regular/Medium

Above: Myriad Pro Regular/Semibold/Bold Condensed

Above: FF Scala

Above: Avenir Light/Roman/Medium/Heavy/Black

GOOD FOR THE HISTORICAL

Chapter 3 suggests turning to history for direction in typeface selection. Even with an idea of which period might be appropriate, there are typefaces that have been designed relatively recently with the intention of reflecting the spirit of a particular time in the past. Let's start with the birth of moveable type (the late-fifteenth century) and progress through to the present day.

Fifteenth and Sixteenth Centuries (Renaissance)

Prior to the birth of moveable type, scripts were calligraphic – letterforms produced with quills or brushes. But new technology that could mould letterforms made way for the thinner lines and refined serifs of Old Style. Typefaces designed recently but based on older faces include Adode's revival of Garamond from the 1980s, Tchichold's Sabon from the 1960s, or Palatino from 1948. Some modern interpretations are even considered to be improvements – more refined versions of their predecessors.

Monotype Bembo	LT Sabon	Bitstream Goudy Old Style
Adobe Jensen	Adobe Garamond	LT Palatino
MT Poliphilus	Adobe Garamond Premier Pro	ITC Cheltenham
Bitstream Aldine 401	LT Plantin	

Above: Bembo Book MT/Italic/Bold/Bold Italic

Above: Garamond Regular/Bold/Bold Italic

Seventeenth and Eighteenth Centuries (Transitional/Neoclassical)

The Enlightenment brought typefaces into the mechanical era. Contrast, colour, drama – these visual themes were evident in the contemporary typefaces of the time, such as Bodoni and Didot from seventeenth-century Italy and France, as they are evident in their modern revisions: Bauer Bodoni from 1926, or Hoefler & Co's Didot from 1991.

Adobe Caslon Pro	Mrs Eaves – Émigré	Adobe Bulmer
MT Baskerville	Adobe Trajan	MT Perpetua
HTF Didot	LT Bodoni	ITC Fenice
MT Fournier	LT Bauer Bodoni	LT Walbaum

Above: Baskerville

Above: Monotype Fournier

Above: Monotype Bulmer

1900s (Romantic)

Romanticism, as expressed by music and literature, explored ideas of love, grief, joy, death and nature. Typography, too, sought to convey the human story. Below are some typefaces designed and/or used during the Romantic era.

LT Plantin

MT Centaur

ATF Copperplate Gothic

Bitstream Goudy Old Style

Guardian Egyptian – Commercial Type

FB Miller

1920s

Several design styles started, converged and overlapped during the early- to mid-twentieth century, responding to the political and industrial developments of the time. The 1920s produced what we now call The New Typography, and also Bauhaus. The typographic layout is how we recognize this movement best, but below are some typefaces the designers of the time would have used in their photo-montaged, asymmetrical compositions, along with typefaces directly inspired by the design thinking of the time.

LT Futura	FF Bau	P22 Albers
Monotype Grotesque	LT Gothic 725	LT Avenir Next
Berthold Akzidenz Grotesk	ARS Region – ARS Type	
LT Venus	P22 Bayer International	**Note:** the typeface ITC Bauhaus was designed in 1975 and has little to do with this era.

1930s

The 1930s were a time of austerity and development. The preceding movements in design had become mainstream and were being used in commerce and marketing. Typography was tasked with communicating en masse (*see* 'Art Deco' on page 247) for an expanded list based on the style only.

MT Gill Sans	LT Peignot	Bell Gothic Bitstream
Berthold Albertus	MT Times New Roman	

Above: Gill Sans Regular/Italic/Bold/Bold Italic

Above: Peignot Light/Demi/Bold

1940s

During and after the Second World War, modern, minimalist designs were now fully accepted as ways to market products. The typefaces used and designed during this time were looking forward, not back (*see* 'Mid-Century' page 248) for an expanded list based on the style only.

LT Trade Gothic

Gotham (H&C)

LT Univers

LT Frutiger

Above: Frutiger Sans & Frutiger Serif.

1950s

Commerce grew as the market for domestic products expanded. Packaging design and advertising were using typefaces with more decorative qualities, used to attract the eye. Today we often associate 'retro' with this era.

LT Optima	Bell Gothic Bitstream	Latin CT
LT Univers	Ed Roman (House Ind.)	House Ind. Brush
LT Helvetica Neue	LT Egyptienne	House Ind. Upright
Adobe Folio	ITC Cheltenham	Lavaderia (LostType Co-op)
Oil Can (LostType Co-op)	URW++ Microgramma	Pompadour Numerals (LostType Co-op)
Compacta (Letraset)	Bitstream Clarendon	

1960s

Prominent designers were now being employed by advertising agencies, and the most notable work of the latter part of the twentieth century is typically commercial. Both minimal and brush-inspired flourished typefaces worked together to attract customers.

LT Sabon	LT Eurostile	ITC Cooper Black
URW Antique Olive	LT Helvetica Neue	Adobe Coronet
MS Calibri	Benguiat Caslon (Photolettering)	Saturn V (LostType Co-op)
A2 Type New Rail Alphabet	Airplane (LostType Co-op)	
ITC Franklin Gothic	Onyx (Bitstream)	

1970s

Below: Avant Garde

Pop art made its way into typographic design during the 1970s, and the output can be seen most frequently on album covers. While rotund, 'party' letterforms advertised fun, serious thinking in postmodern communications continued, and still preferred sans serif typefaces and the stripping down of elements on the page over the old, crowded, embellished designs of the past.

ITC Avant Garde	LT Marconi	Letraset Pump
ITC American Typewriter	Bitstream Bell Centennial	Expressa EF
ITC Bauhaus	Dazzle (Device)	
LT Digi-Grotesk	Blackletter (H. Lubalin)	

1980s

New wave and punk started in earnest in the 1970s, but became prolific the decade after, with another break from tradition – the break of the grid. Text was being dismantled and mixed. The computer also made its debut, and designs began to change very fast (*see* 'Punk' on page 249).

FF Meta	ITC Stone	LT Industria
Apple Chicago	ITC Charter	LT Insignia
URC Lucida Serif	FF Beowolf	Template Gothic
Lucida Sans	LT Rotis	Dead History
Citizen – Émigré	LT Arcadia	Lo Rez – Émigré

1990s

Typeface designs of the 1990s reflect experimentation. With new tools, designers were able to distort, expand, abstract, contort and reinterpret the basic letterforms on which our language is founded. These new letterforms propelled typography to front stage. What was only supporting the message before was now the message itself (*see* 'Grunge' on page 250).

FF Scala	FB Big Caslon	LT Zapfino
Not Caslon – Émigré	LT Auferstehung	Morire
LT Rotis	Adobe Myriad Pro	Keedy Sans – Émigré
Template Gothic – Émigré	MS Trebuchet	FF Erikrighthand
Adobe Jenson	MS Tahoma	FF Justlefthand
	MS Verdana	Matrix II – Émigré
	MT Century Gothic	F2F Hogroach

Jenson

Above: Adobe Jenson Pro

2000s

Typeface design at the start of the twenty-first century began to tire of the novelty made possible by software. Revivals of classic, timeless typefaces were published, and legibility became interesting again. Web design was now something anyone could learn, so typographic decisions were being made by non-professionals, and operating systems provided them with some smart default options.

Mrs Eaves – Émigré

Adobe Garamond Premier Pro

Adobe Trajan Pro

Adobe Hypatia Sans

LT Engravers

MS Calibri

Adobe Cronos

Guardian Egyptian
(Commercial Type)

Klavika (Process Type)

Adobe Warnock Pro

ITC Mekanik

Gotham (H&C)

Neutraface (House Ind.)

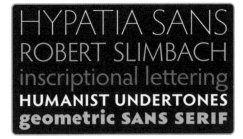

Above: Hypatia Sans Extra Light/Light/Regular/ Bold/Black
Below: Cronos Pro

2010s

The quality typefaces of recent years have focused on melding spirit and legibility, and are often inspired by the specific needs of a particular medium. This approach is not new, but after several decades of type design software being available to the masses, and thus releasing a legion of poorly designed fonts into the world, a fresh appreciation for the skills of the highly trained type designer has returned.

Bree TT

New Rail Alphabet (Photosetting)

Vista Slab – Émigré

2015

It is sometimes difficult to define what is in front of you. Today's typefaces do not always fit into neat categories, but fonts for display seem to be more refined and based on many of the classic genres in preceding pages. A renewed interest in hand-lettering, for example, has inspired typefaces based on vintage painted signage.

What we can be sure of is that with the democratization of type design software, more designers are pursuing type design as a craft, and the output is increasing in quality every year.

Cubano (LostType Co-op)

Edmondsans (LostType Co-op)

Tomasco (LostType Co-op)

Saturn V (LostType Co-op)

On Ramp (LostType Co-op)

Bree TT

OIL CAN

Above: Oil Can

Oil Can

GOOD FOR PERIOD STYLES

Art and design in the 1900s stopped being identified by the time they were conceived, and instead were identified by the ideas they represented. It was the same with typography. The styles were responses to politics, philosophy, economics and industry, fine art, architecture, literature ... Never underestimate the theoretical rigour that went into the design of typefaces.

Victorian

During the Industrial Revolution, printing technology changed for the first time since Gutenberg, and the marketing of products and the birth of mass communication called for big changes in both typeface and graphic design. Fonts got loud. More was more. Here are some typefaces fit for the birth of the commercial age:

Bitstream Modern No. 20	Bitstream Clarendon	Abraham (LostType Co-op)
ITC Modern No. 216	Adobe Birch	Carton (LostType Co-op)

American Woodtype

Similar to the Victorians in England, the US had a need for large letters printable on large-scale posters for advertising. Wood was a practical material for letters of such size. The letterforms changed as a result, and established a style casually called Western.

Adobe Birch	Adobe Blackoak	Adobe Poplar
Adobe Rosewood	Adobe Ironwood	Adobe Zebrawood
LT Engravers	Ranger (LostType Co-op)	ATF Copperplate Gothic
Adobe Cottonwood	Adobe Juniper	Dude Hank Pro (LostType Co-op)
Haymaker (LostType Co-op)	Adobe Mesquite	
Alexis (LostType Co-op)	Adobe Ponderosa	Dude (LostType Co-op)

Art Deco

We are familiar with the graphical and illustration features of Art Deco style. Its fonts took on many of the same characteristics: geometric, bold, verticality, ornamentation, architectural and 'fast'.

BT/Monotype Broadway	LT Futura	BT Parisian
BT Broadway Engraved	Valencia (LostType Co-op)	ITC Luna
URW Broadway Stencil	Vevey (LostType Co-op)	Bitstream Huxley Vertical
LT Peignot	Govenor (LostType Co-op)	Air Ship (LostType Co-op)
New Yorker Type (Wiescher)	ITC Vintage	

Futurist

The Italian Futurists pushed typographic layouts to new extremes. So what were the typefaces they used? Below are several they may have thrown around on a page.

LT Kabel

ITC Bauhaus

ITC Futura

Bertrand Modern

FB Eagle

Adobe Poplar

ITC Franklin Gothic

Berthold City

Below: Broadway

Below: Peignot LT

Below: Eagle Bold

Below: Poplar

Mid-Century

Mid-century modern spanned the 1930s to the 1960s. Typography appropriated the architectural and graphical themes from the Modernist movement: to reject what was and make things new. Some of the features resemble those of Art Deco, with the focus on geometric, structure, aerodynamic shapes, simplicity and urbanism.

Neutraface (House Ind.)	Bitstream Clarendon	ATF Ultra Bodoni
LT Optima	Girard Slab (House Ind.)	FB Nobel
LT Futura Black	Bitstream Profil	MCM Hellenic (Victory)

Modern

Modern typography is usually very passive, in a way that reflects the easy methods of communication that have become prevalent. Simplicity and legibility are the main trends in the fonts below.

LT Avenir	LT Trade Gothic	ITC Franklin Gothic
LT Din Next	LT Univers	

Above: Avenir Light/Roman/Medium/Heavy/Black

Above: Din Next Black/Bold/Ultra Light/Regular/ Medium

Psychedelic

The 1960s changed many things, typography included. The distinctive music posters produced during this time featured letterforms that had been initially drawn, to evoke an altered mind – a reality not confined to the structures put in place by institutions. They were meant to look like feelings.

LT Acid Queen

ITC Neo Neo

Not Caslon – Émigré

Cruz Swinger

Pleasure Point (ComicCraft)

Above: Cruz Swinger

Punk

Also associated with music and rebellion were the 1970s and 1980s – youth disenchanted with conventions and ready to subvert established norms by making their own posters (often cut and pasted). When looking for fonts for punk-esque projects, ask yourself, 'Does this look anarchic?'

Arete Mono – T-26

LT Burnout Chaos

LT Belle

ITC Cyberkugel

LT Dropink

Entebbe LT

Above: ITC Cyberkugel

Grunge

Like the musical genre, grunge fonts represent an important era in the art form's long and esteemed story. Individual expression of angst and rebellion will, of course, extend into how words are printed, and grunge fonts have their place. The importance of context does not stop with the clean, perfected, traditional, even legible, foundations of typography but extends to subversion and experimentation with what it means to communicate. Below are examples of some of the typefaces either developed in the 1980s and 1990s, or ones that express a similar angst, characteristic of that era.

Below: LT Arcadia

LT Arcadia

LT Insignia

LT Industria

FF Blur

Émigré Template Gothic

LT Dropink

LT Not Painted

F2F Styletti LT

F2F Burnout Chaos LT

Adobe Flood

F2F Screen Scream LT

ITC Mekanik

Morire

Below: LT Industria

Below: FF Blur

WILD AND WACKY FONTS

Sometimes, we need a font that defies categorization and speaks louder than any era or style could. The following are goofy, but they have been crafted. And remember your text – yes, context matters, even when designing for something zany. Have fun!

Adobe Mythos

Adobe Strumpf

Letraset Chiller

F2F Hogroach

LT Hollyweird

LT Jambalaya

LT Santa Fe

Not Caslon – Émigré

FF Erikrighthand

FF Justlefthand

Letraset Shatter

Cool Beans – Comicraft

Below: LT Hollyweird Plain

Hollyweird Plain

FURTHER READING

Doh, Jenny, *Creative Lettering*, Lark, 2013

Garfield, Simon, *Just My Type: A Book About Fonts*, Gotham, 2012

Heller, Steven, *100 Ideas that Changed Graphic Design*, Laurence King, 2012

Jaspert, W.P., W. Turner Berry and A.F. Johnson, *Encyclopaedia of Typefaces: The Standard Typography Reference Guide*, Cassell, 2009

Krause, Jim, *Type Idea Index: The Ultimate Designer's Tool for Choosing and Using Fonts Creatively*, How to Design Books, 2007

Lupton, Ellen, *Thinking with Type: A Critical Guide for Designers, Writers, Editors, & Students*, Princeton Architectural Press, 2014

Martin, Keith, Dodd, Robin and Davis, Graham, *1000 Fonts*, Chronicle Books, 2009

Monem, Nadine, *Font: The Sourcebook*, Black Dog Publishing, 2008

Rabie, Solom, *Font Psychology: How Typefaces Affect Our Brains, The power that fonts have on people – Every Designer Must Know*, Solom Rabie, 2015

Stawinski, Gregor, *Retro Fonts*, Laurence King, 2010

Seddon, Tony, *Draw Your Own Fonts: 30 Alphabets to Scribble, Sketch and Make Your Own*, Ivy Press, 2013

Walters, John L, *Fifty Typefaces That Changed the World*, Conran, 2013

Young, Doyald, *Fonts & Logos: Font Analysis, Logotype Design, Typography, Type Comparison*, Delphi Pub, 1999

USEFUL WEBSITES

creativebloq.com

With a great many articles, tips and tricks, not to mention frequent font giveaways, Creative Bloq is a useful website to check in on frequently if you want to keep on top of everything going on in typographical design.

ilovetypography.com

A fantastic blog covering everything you can think of about typography, with a huge archive of treasured articles. A particular favourite is the entry, 'Unusual fifteenth-century fonts.'

fonts.info

A great place for graphic designers to find new fonts.

fontsquirrel.com

A great source of free fonts for anyone looking to expand their font collection. A brilliant site that's very easy to use.

graphicdesign.stackexchange.com

Do you have a burning question that you just can't find the answer to? Graphic Design Stack Exchange might be the place for you. It's a budding community of graphic design professionals, graphic design students and enthusiasts asking and answering questions.

howdesign.com

A popular site with all of those interested in the professional design world. This site will be most useful to you if you are working as a designer, or if you want to soon.

thedsgnblog.com

As the design blog says, 'Don't just be a designer, be a good one.' This is the best place to go if you are a recent graphic design graduate looking for posts about young designers and students to inspire and encourage you.

typographica.org

Lots of reviews and commentary about everything going on in the typographical world at the moment.

typography-daily.com

A daily dose of typographical inspiration, particularly for those interested in viewing and engaging in experimentations with font art.

typographyserved.com

Typography Served features powerful typographical artworks, including typeface design, lettering and illustrated typography.

www.youtube.com/watch?v=wOgIkxAfJsk

This is an animated short video on the history of typography. A definite must-watch if you want to learn lots about the history of fonts in under five minutes.

INDEX